ABRAHAM

LINCOLN'S

HUMOROUS STORIES

Compiled

By

Alexander K. McClure

Abraham Lincoln's Humorous Stories
By Alexander K. McClure

Copyright © 2006 by El Paso Norte Press
All rights reserved. No part of this book may be reproduced or utilized in any form or by any means, electronic or mechanical, including photocopying, recording, or by any information storage and retrieval system, without permission in writing from the publisher, except that brief passages may be quoted by reviewers provided full credit is given.

First Edition – January 2006

Published by
EL Paso Norte Press
404 Christopher Ave
El Paso, Texas 79912

ISBN 0-9773400-9-0

Printed in the United States of America

PREFACE

Whenever Abraham Lincoln wanted to make a strong point he usually began by saying, "Now, that reminds me of a story." And when he had told a story every one saw the point and was put into a good humor.

Before Lincoln was ever heard of as a lawyer or politician, he was famous as a story teller. As a politician, he always had a story to fit the other side; as a lawyer, he won many cases by telling the jury a story which showed them the justice of his side better than any argument could have done.

While nearly all of Lincoln's stories have a humorous side, they also contain a moral, which every good story should have. They contain lessons that could be taught so well in no other way. Every one of them is a sermon. Lincoln, like the Man of Galilee, spoke to the people in parables.

Nothing that can be written about Lincoln can show his character in such a true light as the yarns and stories he was so fond of telling, and at which he would laugh as heartily as anyone. For a man whose life was so full of great responsibilities, Lincoln had many hours of laughter when the humorous, fun-loving side of his great nature asserted itself.

Every person to keep healthy ought to have one good hearty laugh every day. Lincoln did, and the stories at which he laughed will continue to furnish laughter to all who appreciate good humor, with a moral point and spiced with that true philosophy bred in those who live close to nature and to the people around them.

The parables, yarns, stories, anecdotes and sayings of the "Immortal Abe" deserve a place beside Aesop's Fables, Bunyan's Pilgrim's Progress and all other books that have added to the happiness and wisdom of mankind. Lincoln's stories are like Lincoln himself. The more we know of them the better we like them.

ABRAHAM LINCOLN'S HUMOROUS STORIES

HIS FINANCIAL STANDING

A New York firm applied to Abraham Lincoln, some years before he became President, for information as to the financial standing of one of his neighbors. Mr. Lincoln replied:

"I am well acquainted with Mr.-- and know his circumstances. First of all, he has a wife and baby; together they ought to be worth $50,000 to any man. Secondly, he has an office in which there is a table worth $1.50 and three chairs worth, say, $1. Last of all, there is in one corner a large rat hole, which will bear looking into.
Respectfully, A. Lincoln"

THE DANDY AND THE BOYS

President Lincoln appointed as consul to a South American country a young man from Ohio who was a dandy. A wag met the new appointee on his way to the White House to thank the President. He was dressed in the most extravagant style. The wag horrified him by telling him that the country to which he was assigned was noted chiefly for the bugs that abounded there and made life unbearable.

"They'll bore a hole clean through you before a week has passed," was the comforting assurance of the wag as they parted at the White House steps. The new consul approached Lincoln with disappointment clearly written all over his face. Instead of joyously thanking the President, he told him the wag's story of the bugs. "I am informed, Mr. President," he said, "that the place is full of vermin and that they could eat me up in a week's time." "Well, young man," replied Lincoln, "if that's true, all I've got to say is that if such a thing happened they would leave a mighty good suit of clothes behind."

LINCOLN ASKED TO BE SHOT

Lincoln was, naturally enough, much surprised one day, when a man of rather forbidding countenance drew a revolver and thrust the weapon almost into his face. In such circumstances "Abe" at once concluded that any attempt at debate or argument was a waste of time and words.

"What seems to be the matter?" inquired Lincoln with all the calmness and self-possession he could muster.

"Well," replied the stranger, who did not appear at all excited, "some years ago I swore an oath that if I ever came across an uglier man than myself I'd shoot him on the spot."

A feeling of relief evidently took possession of Lincoln at this rejoinder, as the expression upon his countenance lost all suggestion of anxiety.

"Shoot me," he said to the stranger; "for if I am an uglier man than you I don't want to live."

"I'VE LOST MY APPLE"

During a public "reception," a farmer from one of the border counties of Virginia told the President that the Union soldiers, in passing his farm, had helped themselves not only to hay, but his horse, and he hoped the President would urge the proper officer to consider his claim immediately.

Mr. Lincoln said that this reminded him of an old acquaintance of his, "Jack" Chase, a lumberman on the Illinois, a steady, sober man, and the best raftsman on the river. It was quite a trick to take the logs over the rapids; but he was skilful with a raft, and always kept her straight in the channel. Finally a steamer was put on, and "Jack" was made captain of her. He always used to take the wheel, going through the rapids. One day when the boat was plunging and wallowing along the boiling current, and "Jack's" utmost vigilance was being exercised to keep her in the narrow channel, a boy pulled his coat-tail and hailed him with:

"Say, Mister Captain! I wish you would just stop your boat a minute-- I've lost my apple overboard!"

TIME LOST DIDN'T COUNT

Thurlow Weed, the veteran journalist and politician, once related how, when he was opposing the claims of Montgomery Blair, who aspired to a Cabinet appointment, that Mr. Lincoln inquired of Mr. Weed whom he would recommend, "Henry Winter Davis," was the response.

"David Davis, I see, has been posting you up on this question," retorted Lincoln. "He has Davis on the brain. I think Maryland must be a good State to move from."

The President then told a story of a witness in court in a neighboring county, who, on being asked his age, replied, "Sixty." Being satisfied he was much older the question was repeated, and on receiving the same answer the court admonished the witness, saying, "The court knows you to be much older than sixty."

"Oh, I understand now," was the rejoinder, "you're thinking of those ten years I spent on the eastern share of Maryland; that was so much time lost, and didn't count."

Blair was made Postmaster-General.

NO VICES, NO VIRTUES

Lincoln always took great pleasure in relating this yarn:

Riding at one time in a stage with an old Kentuckian who was returning from Missouri, Lincoln excited the old gentleman's surprise by refusing to accept either of tobacco or French brandy.

When they separated that afternoon--the Kentuckian to take another stage bound for Louisville--he shook hands warmly with Lincoln, and said, good-humoredly:

"See here, stranger, you're a clever but strange companion. I may never see you again, and I don't want to offend you, but I want to say this: My experience has taught me that a man who has no vices has damned few virtues. Good-day."

LINCOLN'S DUES

Miss Todd (afterwards Mrs. Lincoln) had a keen sense of the ridiculous, and wrote several articles in the Springfield (Ill.) "Journal" reflecting severely upon General James Shields (who won fame in the Mexican and Civil Wars, and was United States Senator from three states), then Auditor of State.

Lincoln assumed the authorship, and was challenged by Shields to meet him on the "field of honor." Meanwhile Miss Todd increased Shields' ire by writing another letter to the paper, in which she said: "I hear the way of these fire-eaters is to give the challenged party the choice of weapons, which being the case, I'll tell you in confidence that I never fight with anything but broom-sticks, or hot water, or a shovelful of coals, the former of which, being somewhat like a shillelagh, may not be objectionable to him."

Lincoln accepted the challenge, and selected broadswords as the weapons. Judge Herndon (Lincoln's law partner) gives the closing of this affair as follows

"The laws of Illinois prohibited dueling, and Lincoln demanded that the meeting should be outside the state. Shields undoubtedly knew that Lincoln was opposed to fighting a duel--that his moral sense would revolt at the thought, and that he would not be likely to break the law by fighting in the state. Possibly he thought Lincoln would make a humble apology. Shields was brave, but foolish, and would not listen to overtures for explanation. It was arranged that the meeting should be in Missouri, opposite Alton. "They proceeded to the place selected, but friends interfered, and there was no duel. There is little doubt that the man who had swung a beetle and driven iron wedges into gnarled hickory logs could have cleft the skull of his antagonist, but he had no such intention. He repeatedly said to the friends of Shields that in writing the first article he had no thought of anything personal. The Auditor's vanity had been sorely wounded by the second letter, in regard to which Lincoln could not make any explanation except that he had had no hand in writing it. The affair set all Springfield to laughing at Shields."

"DONE WITH THE BIBLE"

A country meeting-house, that was used once a month, was quite a distance from any other house.

The preacher, an old-line Baptist, was dressed in coarse linen pantaloons, and shirt of the same material. The pants, manufactured after the old fashion, with baggy legs, and a flap in the front, were made to attach to his frame without the aid of suspenders.

A single button held his shirt in position, and that was at the collar. He rose up in the pulpit, and with a loud voice announced his text thus: "I am the Christ whom I shall represent to-day."

About this time a little blue lizard ran up his roomy pantaloons. The old preacher, not wishing to interrupt the steady flow of his sermon, slapped away on his leg, expecting to arrest the intruder, but his efforts were unavailing, and the little fellow kept on ascending higher and higher.

Continuing the sermon, the preacher loosened the central button which graced the waistband of his pantaloons, and with a kick off came that easy fitting garment.

But, meanwhile, Mr. Lizard had passed the equatorial line of the waistband, and was calmly exploring that part of the preacher's anatomy which lay underneath the back of his shirt.

Things were now growing interesting, but the sermon was still grinding on. The next movement on the preacher's part was for the collar button, and with one sweep of his arm off came the tow linen shirt.

The congregation sat for an instant as if dazed; at length one old lady in the rear part of the room rose up, and, glancing at the excited object in the pulpit, shouted at the top of her voice: "If you represent Christ, then I'm done with the Bible."

HIS KNOWLEDGE OF HUMAN NATURE

Once, when Lincoln was pleading a case, the opposing lawyer had all the advantage of the law; the weather was warm, and his opponent, as was admissible in frontier courts, pulled off his coat and vest as he grew warm in the argument.

At that time, shirts with buttons behind were unusual. Lincoln took in the situation at once. Knowing the prejudices of the primitive people against pretension of all sorts, or any affectation of superior social rank, arising, he said: "Gentlemen of the jury, having justice on my side, I don't think you will be at all influenced by the gentleman's pretended knowledge of the law, when you see he does not even know which side of his shirt should be in front." There was a general laugh, and Lincoln's case was won.

A MISCHIEVOUS OX

President Lincoln once told the following story of Colonel W., who had been elected to the Legislature, and had also been judge of the

County Court. His elevation, however, had made him somewhat pompous, and he became very fond of using big words. On his farm he had a very large and mischievous ox, called "Big Brindle," which very frequently broke down his neighbors' fences, and committed other depredations, much to the Colonel's annoyance.

One morning after breakfast, in the presence of Lincoln, who had stayed with him over night, and who was on his way to town, he called his overseer and said to him:

"Mr. Allen, I desire you to impound 'Big Brindle,' in order that I may hear no animadversions on his eternal depredations,"

Allen bowed and walked off, sorely puzzled to know what the Colonel wanted him to do. After Colonel W. left for town, he went to his wife and asked her what the Colonel meant by telling him to impound the ox.

"Why, he meant to tell you to put him in a pen," said she.

Allen left to perform the feat, for it was no inconsiderable one, as the animal was wild and vicious, but, after a great deal of trouble and vexation, succeeded.

"Well," said he, wiping the perspiration from his brow and soliloquizing, "this is impounding, is it? Now, I am dead sure that the Colonel will ask me if I impounded 'Big Brindle,' and I'll bet I puzzle him as he did me."

The next day the Colonel gave a dinner party, and as he was not aristrocratic, Allen, the overseer, sat down with the company. After the second or third glass was discussed, the Colonel turned to the overseer and said

"Eh, Mr. Allen, did you impound 'Big Brindle,' sir?"

Allen straightened himself, and looking around at the company, replied:

"Yes, I did, sir; but 'Old Brindle' transcended the impannel of the impound, and scatterlophisticated all over the equanimity of the forest."

The company burst into an immoderate fit of laughter, while the Colonel's face reddened with discomfiture.

"What do you mean by that, sir?" demanded the Colonel.

"Why, I mean, Colonel," replied Allen, "that 'Old Brindle,' being prognosticated with an idea of the cholera, ripped and teared, snorted and pawed dirt, jumped the fence, tuck to the woods, and would not be impounded nohow."

This was too much; the company roared again, the Colonel being forced to join in the laughter, and in the midst of the jollity Allen left the table, saying to himself as he went, "I reckon the Colonel won't ask me to impound any more oxen."

THE PRESIDENTIAL "CHIN-FLY"

Some of Mr. Lincoln's intimate friends once called his attention to a certain member of his Cabinet who was quietly working to secure a nomination for the Presidency, although knowing that Mr. Lincoln was to be a candidate for re-election. His friends insisted that the Cabinet officer ought to be made to give up his Presidential aspirations or be removed from office. The situation reminded Mr. Lincoln of a story:

"My brother and I," he said, "were once plowing corn, I driving the horse and he holding the plow. The horse was lazy, but on one occasion he rushed across the field so that I, with my long legs, could scarcely keep pace with him. On reaching the end of the furrow, I found an enormous chin-fly fastened upon him, and knocked him off. My brother asked me what I did that for. I told him I didn't want the old horse bitten in that way. 'Why,' said my brother, 'that's all that made him go.' Now," said Mr. Lincoln, "if Mr.-- has a Presidential chin-fly biting him, I'm not going to knock him off, if it will only make his department go."

'SQUIRE BAGLY'S PRECEDENT

Mr. T. W. S. Kidd, of Springfield, says that he once heard a lawyer opposed to Lincoln trying to convince a jury that precedent was superior to law, and that custom made things legal in all cases. When Lincoln arose to answer him he told the jury he would argue his case in the same way.

"Old 'Squire Bagly, from Menard, came into my office and said, 'Lincoln, I want your advice as a lawyer. Has a man what's been elected justice of the peace a right to issue a marriage license?' I told him he had not; when the old 'squire threw himself back in his chair very indignantly, and said, 'Lincoln, I thought you was a lawyer. Now Bob Thomas and me had a bet on this thing, and we agreed to let you decide; but if this is your opinion I don't want it, for I know a thunderin' sight better, for I have been 'squire now for eight years and have done it all the time.'"

HE'D NEED HIS GUN

When the President, early in the War, was anxious about the defenses of Washington, he told a story illustrating his feelings in the case. General Scott, then Commander-in-Chief of the United States Army, had but 1,500 men, two guns and an old sloop of war, the latter anchored in the Potomac, with which to protect the National Capital, and the President was uneasy.

To one of his queries as to the safety of Washington, General Scott had replied, "It has been ordained, Mr. President, that the city shall not be captured by the Confederates."

"But we ought to have more men and guns here," was the Chief Executive's answer. "The Confederates are not such fools as to let a good chance to capture Washington go by, and even if it has been ordained that the city is safe, I'd feel easier if it were better protected. All this reminds me of the old trapper out in the West who had been assured by some 'city folks' who had hired him as a guide that all matters regarding life and death were prearranged.

"'It is ordained,' said one of the party to the old trapper, 'that you are to die at a certain time, and no one can kill you before that time. If you met a thousand Indians, and your death had not been ordained for that day, you would certainly escape.'

"'I don't exactly understand this "ordained" business,' was the trapper's reply. 'I don't care to run no risks. I always have my gun with me, so that if I come across some reds I can feel sure that I won't cross the Jordan 'thout taking some of 'em with me. Now, for instance, if I met an Indian in the woods; he drew a bead on me--sayin', too, that he wasn't more'n ten feet away--an' I didn't have nothing to protect myself; say it was as bad as that, the redskin bein' dead ready to kill me; now, even if it had been ordained that the Indian (sayin' he was a good shot), was to die that very minute, an' I wasn't, what would I do 'thout my gun?'

"There you are," the President remarked; "even if it has been ordained that the city of Washington will never be taken by the Southerners, what would we do in case they made an attack upon the place, without men and heavy guns?"

KEPT UP THE ARGUMENT

Judge T. Lyle Dickey of Illinois related that when the excitement over the Kansas Nebraska bill first broke out, he was with Lincoln and several friends attending court. One evening several persons, including himself and Lincoln, were discussing the slavery question. Judge Dickey contended that slavery was an institution which the Constitution recognized, and which could not be disturbed. Lincoln argued that ultimately slavery must become extinct. "After awhile," said Judge Dickey, "we went upstairs to bed. There were two beds in our room, and I remember that Lincoln sat up in his night shirt on the edge of the bed arguing the point with me. At last we went to sleep. Early in the morning I woke up and there was Lincoln half sitting up in bed. 'Dickey,' said he, 'I tell you this nation cannot exist half slave and half free.' 'Oh, Lincoln,' said I, 'go to sleep.'"

EQUINE INGRATITUDE

President Lincoln, while eager that the United States troops should be supplied with the most modern and serviceable weapons, often took occasion to put his foot down upon the mania for experimenting with which some of his generals were afflicted. While engaged in these experiments much valuable time was wasted, the enemy was left to do as he thought best, no battles were fought, and opportunities for winning victories allowed to pass.

The President was an exceedingly practical man, and when an invention, idea or discovery was submitted to him, his first step was to ascertain how any or all of them could be applied in a way to be of benefit to the army. As to experimenting with "contrivances" which, to his mind, could never be put to practical use, he had little patience.

"Some of these generals," said he, "experiment so long and so much with newfangled, fancy notions that when they are finally brought to a head they are useless. Either the time to use them has gone by, or the machine, when put in operation, kills more than it cures.

"One of these generals, who has a scheme for 'condensing' rations, is willing to swear his life away that his idea, when carried to perfection, will reduce the cost of feeding the Union troops to almost nothing, while the soldiers themselves will get so fat that they'll 'bust out' of their uniforms. Of course, uniforms cost nothing, and real fat men are more active and vigorous than lean, skinny ones, but that is getting away from my story.

"There was once an Irishman--a cabman--who had a notion that he could induce his horse to live entirely on shavings. The latter he could get for nothing, while corn and oats were pretty high-priced. So he daily lessened the amount of food to the horse, substituting shavings for the corn and oats abstracted, so that the horse wouldn't know his rations were being cut down.

"However, just as he had achieved success in his experiment, and the horse had been taught to live without other food than shavings, the ungrateful animal 'up and died,' and he had to buy another.

"So far as this general referred to is concerned, I'm afraid the soldiers will all be dead at the time when his experiment is demonstrated as thoroughly successful."

'TWAS "MOVING DAY"

Speed, who was a prosperous young merchant of Springfield, reports that Lincoln's personal effects consisted of a pair of saddle-bags, containing two or three lawbooks, and a few pieces of clothing. Riding on a borrowed horse, he thus made his appearance in Springfield. When he discovered that a single bedstead would cost seventeen dollars he said, "It is probably cheap enough, but I have not enough money to pay for it." When Speed offered to trust him, he said: "If I fail here as a lawyer, I will probably never pay you at all." Then Speed offered to share large double bed with him.

"Where is your room?" Lincoln asked.

"Upstairs," said Speed, pointing from the store leading to his room.

Without saying a word, he took his saddle-bags on his arm, went upstairs, set them down on the floor, came down again, and with a face beaming with pleasure and smiles, exclaimed: "Well, Speed, I'm moved."

"ABE'S" HAIR NEEDED COMBING

"By the way," remarked President Lincoln one day to Colonel Cannon, a close personal friend, "I can tell you a good story about my hair. When I was nominated at Chicago, an enterprising fellow thought that a great many people would like to see how 'Abe' Lincoln looked, and, as I had not long before sat for a photograph, the fellow, having seen it, rushed over and bought the negative.

"He at once got no end of wood-cuts, and so active was their circulation they were soon selling in all parts of the country.

"Soon after they reached Springfield, I heard a boy crying them for sale on the streets. 'Here's your likeness of "Abe" Lincoln!' he shouted. 'Buy one; price only two shillings! Will look a great deal better when he gets his hair combed!'"

WOULD "TAKE TO THE WOODS"

Secretary of State Seward was bothered considerably regarding the complication into which Spain had involved the United States government in connection with San Domingo, and related his troubles to the President. Negotiations were not proceeding satisfactorily, and things were mixed generally. We wished to conciliate Spain, while the negroes had appealed against Spanish oppression.

The President did not, to all appearances, look at the matter seriously, but, instead of treating the situation as a grave one, remarked that Seward's dilemma reminded him of an interview between two negroes in Tennessee.

One was a preacher, who, with the crude and strange notions of his ignorant race, was endeavoring to admonish and enlighten his brother African of the importance of religion and the danger of the future.

"Dar are," said Josh, the preacher, "two roads befo' you, Joe; be ca'ful which ob dese you take. Narrow am de way dat leads straight to destruction; but broad am de way dat leads right to damnation."

Joe opened his eyes with affright, and under the spell of the awful danger before him, exclaimed, "Josh, take which road you please; I shall go troo de woods."

"I am not willing," concluded the President, "to assume any new troubles or responsibilities at this time, and shall therefore avoid going to the one place with Spain, or with the negro to the other, but shall 'take to the woods.' We will maintain an honest and strict neutrality."

BOAT HAD TO STOP

Lincoln never failed to take part in all political campaigns in Illinois, as his reputation as a speaker caused his services to be in great demand. As was natural, he was often the target at which many of the "Smart Alecks" of that period shot their feeble bolts, but Lincoln was so ready with his answers that few of them cared to engage him a second time.

In one campaign Lincoln was frequently annoyed by a young man who entertained the idea that he was a born orator. He had a loud voice, was full of language, and so conceited that he could not understand why the people did not recognize and appreciate his abilities.

This callow politician delighted in interrupting public speakers, and at last Lincoln determined to squelch him. One night while addressing a large meeting at Springfield, the fellow became so offensive that "Abe" dropped the threads of his speech and turned his attention to the tormentor.

"I don't object," said Lincoln, "to being interrupted with sensible questions, but I must say that my boisterous friend does not always make inquiries which properly come under that head. He says he is afflicted with headaches, at which I don't wonder, as it is a well-known fact that nature abhors a vacuum, and takes her own way of demonstrating it.

"This noisy friend reminds me of a certain steamboat that used to run on the Illinois river. It was an energetic boat, was always busy. When they built it, however, they made one serious mistake, this error being in the relative sizes of the boiler and the whistle. The latter was usually busy, too, and people were aware that it was in existence.

"This particular boiler to which I have reference was a six-foot one, and did all that was required of it in the way of pushing the boat along; but as the builders of the vessel had made the whistle a six-foot one, the consequence was that every time the whistle blew the boat had to stop."

MCCLELLAN'S "SPECIAL TALENT"

President Lincoln one day remarked to a number of personal friends who had called upon him at the White House:

"General McClellan's tardiness and unwillingness to fight the enemy or follow up advantages gained, reminds me of a man back in Ilinois who knew a few law phrases but whose lawyer lacked aggressiveness. The man finally lost all patience and springing to his feet vociferated, 'Why don't you go at him with a fi. fa., a demurrer, a capias, a surrebutter, or a ne exeat, or something; or a nundam pactum or a non est?'

"I wish McClellan would go at the enemy with something--I don't care what. General McClellan is a pleasant and scholarly gentleman. He is an admirable engineer, but he seems to have a special talent for a stationary engine."

MORE LIGHT AND LESS NOISE

The President was bothered to death by those persons who boisterously demanded that the War be pushed vigorously; also, those who shouted their advice and opinions into his weary ears, but who never suggested anything practical. These fellows were not in the army, nor did they ever take any interest, in a personal way, in military matters, except when engaged in dodging drafts.

"That reminds me," remarked Mr. Lincoln one day, "of a farmer who lost his way on the Western frontier. Night came on, and the embarrassments of his position were increased by a furious tempest which suddenly burst upon him. To add to his discomfort, his horse had given out, leaving him exposed to all the dangers of the pitiless storm.

"The peals of thunder were terrific, the frequent flashes of lightning affording the only guide on the road as he resolutely trudged onward, leading his jaded steed. The earth seemed fairly to tremble beneath him in the war of elements. One bolt threw him suddenly upon his knees.

"Our traveler was not a prayerful man, but finding himself involuntarily brought to an attitude of devotion, he addressed himself to the Throne of Grace in the following prayer for his deliverance

"'O God! hear my prayer this time, for Thou knowest it is not often that I call upon Thee. And, O Lord! if it is all the same to Thee, give us a little more light and a little less noise.'

"I wish," the President said, sadly, "there was a stronger disposition manifested on the part of our civilian warriors to unite in suppressing the rebellion, and a little less noise as to how and by whom the chief executive office shall be administered."

ONE BULLET AND A HATFUL

Lincoln made the best of everything, and if he couldn't get what he wanted he took what he could get. In matters of policy, while President he acted according to this rule. He would take perilous chances, even when the result was, to the minds of his friends, not worth the risk he had run.

One day at a meeting of the Cabinet, it being at the time when it seemed as though war with England and France could not be avoided, Secretary of State Seward and Secretary of War Stanton warmly advocated that the United States maintain an attitude, the result of which would have been a declaration of hostilities by the European Powers mentioned.

"Why take any more chances than are absolutely necessary?" asked the President.

"We must maintain our honor at any cost," insisted Secretary Seward.

"We would be branded as cowards before the entire world," Secretary Stanton said.

"But why run the greater risk when we can take a smaller one?" queried the President calmly. "The less risk we run the better for us. That reminds me of a story I heard a day or two ago, the hero of which was on the firing line during a recent battle, where the bullets were flying thick.

"Finally his courage gave way entirely, and throwing down his gun, he ran for dear life.

"As he was flying along at top speed he came across an officer who drew his revolver and shouted, 'Go back to your regiment at once or I will shoot you!'

"'Shoot and be hanged,' the racer exclaimed. 'What's one bullet to a whole hatful?'"

LINCOLN'S STORY TO PEACE COMMISSIONERS

Among the reminiscences of Lincoln left by Editor Henry J. Raymond, is the following:

Among the stories told by Lincoln, which is freshest in my mind, one which he related to me shortly after its occurrence, belongs to the history of the famous interview on board the River Queen, at Hampton Roads, between himself and Secretary Seward and the rebel Peace Commissioners. It was reported at the time that the President told a "little story" on that occasion, and the inquiry went around among the newspapers, "What was it?"

The New York Herald published what purported to be a version of it, but the "point" was entirely lost, and it attracted no attention. Being in Washington a few days subsequent to the interview with the Commissioners (my previous sojourn there having terminated about the first of last August), I asked Mr. Lincoln one day if it was true that he told Stephens, Hunter and Campbell a story.

"Why, yes," he replied, manifesting some surprise, "but has it leaked out? I was in hopes nothing would be said about it, lest some over-sensitive people should imagine there was a degree of levity in the intercourse between us." He then went on to relate the circumstances which called it out.

"You see," said he, "we had reached and were discussing the slavery question. Mr. Hunter said, substantially, that the slaves, always accustomed to an overseer, and to work upon compulsion, suddenly freed, as they would be if the South should consent to peace on the basis of the 'Emancipation Proclamation,' would precipitate not only themselves, but the entire Southern society, into irremediable ruin. No work would be done, nothing would be cultivated, and both blacks and whites would starve!"

Said the President: "I waited for Seward to answer that argument, but as he was silent, I at length said: 'Mr. Hunter, you ought to know a great deal better about this argument than I, for you have always lived under the slave system. I can only say, in reply to your statement of the case, that it reminds me of a man out in Illinois, by the name of Case, who undertook, a few years ago, to raise a very large herd of hogs. It was a great trouble to feed them, and how to get around this was a puzzle to him. At length he hit on the plan of planting an immense field of potatoes, and, when they were sufficiently grown, he turned the whole herd into the field, and let them have full swing, thus saving not only the labor of feeding the hogs, but also that of digging the potatoes. Charmed with his sagacity, he stood one day leaning against the fence, counting his hogs, when a neighbor came along.

"'Well, well,' said he, 'Mr. Case, this is all very fine. Your hogs are doing very well just now, but you know out here in Illinois the frost comes early, and the ground freezes for a foot deep. Then what you going to do?'

"This was a view of the matter which Mr. Case had not taken into account. Butchering time for hogs was 'way on in December or January! He scratched his head, and at length stammered: 'Well, it may come pretty hard on their snouts, but I don't see but that it will be "root, hog, or die."'"

"ABE" GOT THE WORST OF IT

When Lincoln was a young lawyer in Illinois, he and a certain Judge once got to bantering one another about trading horses; and it was agreed that the next morning at nine o'clock they should make a trade, the horses to be unseen up to that hour, and no backing out, under a forfeiture of $25. At the hour appointed, the Judge came up, leading the sorriest-looking specimen of a horse ever seen in those parts. In a few minutes Mr. Lincoln was seen approaching with a wooden saw-horse upon his shoulders.

Great were the shouts and laughter of the crowd, and both were greatly increased when Lincoln, on surveying the Judge's animal, set down his saw-horse, and exclaimed:

"Well, Judge, this is the first time I ever got the worst of it in a horse trade."

IT DEPENDED UPON HIS CONDITION

The President had made arrangements to visit New York, and was told that President Garrett, of the Baltimore and Ohio Railroad, would be glad to furnish a special train.

"I don't doubt it a bit," remarked the President, "for I know Mr. Garrett, and like him very well, and if I believed--which I don't, by any means--all the things some people say about his 'secesh' principles, he might say to you as was said by the Superintendent of a certain railroad to a son of one my predecessors in office. Some two years after the death of President Harrison, the son of his successor in this office wanted to take his father on an excursion somewhere or other, and went to the Superintendent's office to order a special train.

"This Superintendent was a Whig of the most uncompromising sort, who hated a Democrat more than all other things on the earth, and promptly refused the young man's request, his language being to the effect that this particular railroad was not running special trains for the accommodation of Presidents of the United States just at that season.

"The son of the President was much surprised and exceedingly annoyed. 'Why,' he said, 'you have run special Presidential trains, and I know it. Didn't you furnish a special train for the funeral of President Harrison?'

"'Certainly we did,' calmly replied the Superintendent, with no relaxation of his features, 'and if you will only bring your father here in the same shape as General Harrison was, you shall have the best train on the road.'"

When the laughter had subsided, the President said: "I shall take pleasure in accepting Mr. Garrett's offer, as I have no doubts whatever as to his loyalty to the United States government or his respect for the occupant of the Presidential office."

"GOT DOWN TO THE RAISINS"

A. B. Chandler, chief of the telegraph office at the War Department, occupied three rooms, one of which was called "the President's room," so much of his time did Mr. Lincoln spend there. Here he would read over the telegrams received for the several heads of departments. Three copies of all messages received were made--one for the President, one for the War Department records and one for Secretary Stanton.

Mr. Chandler told a story as to the manner in which the President read the despatches:

"President Lincoln's copies were kept in what we called the 'President's drawer' of the 'cipher desk.' He would come in at any time of the night or day, and go at once to this drawer, and take out a file of telegrams, and begin at the top to read them. His position in running over these telegrams was sometimes very curious.

"He had a habit of sitting frequently on the edge of his chair, with his right knee dragged down to the floor. I remember a curious expression of his when he got to the bottom of the new telegrams and began on those that he had read before. It was, 'Well, I guess I have got down to the raisins.'

"The first two or three times he said this he made no explanation, and I did not ask one. But one day, after he had made the remark, he looked up under his eyebrows at me with a funny twinkle in his eyes, and said: 'I used to know a little girl out West who sometimes was inclined to eat too much. One day she ate a good many more raisins than she ought to, and followed them up with a quantity of other goodies. They made her very sick. After a time the raisins began to come.

"She gasped and looked at her mother and said: 'Well, I will be better now I guess, for I have got down to the raisins.'"

SAVING HIS WIND

Judge H. W. Beckwith of Danville, Ill., said that soon after the Ottawa debate between Lincoln and Douglas he passed the Chenery House, then the principal hotel in Springfield. The lobby was crowded with partisan leaders from various sections of the state, and Mr. Lincoln, from his greater height, was seen above the surging mass that clung about him like a swarm of bees to their ruler. The day was warm, and at the first chance he broke away and came out for a little fresh air, wiping the sweat from his face.

"As he passed the door he saw me," said Judge Beckwith, "and, taking my hand, inquired for the health and views of his 'friends over in Vermillion county.' He was assured they were wide awake, and further told that they looked forward to the debate between him and Senator Douglas with deep concern. From the shadow that went quickly over his face, the pained look that came to give way quickly to a blaze of eyes and quiver of lips, I felt that Mr. Lincoln had gone beneath my mere words and caught my inner and current fears as to the result. And then, in a forgiving, jocular way peculiar to him, he said: 'Sit down; I have a moment to spare, and will tell you a story.' Having been on his feet for some time, he sat on the end of the stone step leading into the hotel door, while I stood closely fronting him.

" You have,' he continued, 'seen two men about to fight?'

"'Yes, many times.'

"'Well, one of them brags about what he means to do. He jumps high in the air, cracking his heels together, smites his fists, and wastes his wreath trying to scare somebody. You see the other fellow, he says not a word,'--here Mr. Lincoln's voice and manner changed to great earnestness, and repeating--'you see the other man says not a word. His arms are at his sides, his fists are closely doubled up, his head is drawn to the shoulder, and his teeth are set firm together. He is saving his wind for the fight, and as sure as it comes off he will win it, or die a-trying.'"

RIGHT FOR, ONCE, ANYHOW

Where men bred in courts, accustomed to the world, or versed in diplomacy, would use some subterfuge, or would make a polite speech, or give a shrug of the shoulders, as the means of getting out of an embarrassing position, Lincoln raised a laugh by some bold west-country anecdote, and moved off in the cloud of merriment produced by the joke. When Attorney-General Bates was remonstrating apparently against the appointment of some indifferent lawyer to a place of judicial importance, the President interposed with: "Come now, Bates, he's not half as bad as you think. Besides that, I must tell you, he did me a good turn long ago. When I took to the law, I was going to court one morning, with some ten or twelve miles of bad road before me, and I had no horse.

"The judge overtook me in his carriage.

"'Hallo, Lincoln! are you not going to the court-house? Come in and I will give you a seat!'

"Well, I got in, and the Judge went on reading his papers. Presently the carriage struck a stump on one side of the road, then it hopped off to the other. I looked out, and I saw the driver was jerking from side to side in his seat, so I says

"'Judge, I think your coachman has been taking a little too much this morning.'

"'Well, I declare, Lincoln,' said he, 'I should not much wonder if you were right, for he has nearly upset me half a dozen times since starting.'

"So, putting his head out of the window, he shouted, 'Why, you infernal scoundrel, you are drunk!'

"Upon which, pulling up his horses, and turning round with great gravity, the coachman said:

"'Begorra! that's the first rightful decision that you have given for the last twelvemonth.'"

While the company were laughing, the President beat a quiet retreat from the neighborhood.

"PITY THE POOR ORPHAN"

After the War was well on, and several battles had been fought, a lady from Alexandria asked the President for an order to release a certain church which had been taken for a Federal hospital. The President said he could do nothing, as the post surgeon at Alexandria was immovable, and then asked the lady why she did not donate money to build a hospital.

"We have been very much embarrassed by the war," she replied, "and our estates are much hampered."

"You are not ruined?" asked the President.

"No, sir, but we do not feel that we should give up anything we have left."

The President, after some reflection, then said: "There are more battles yet to be fought, and I think God would prefer that your church be devoted to the care and alleviation of the sufferings of our poor fellows. So, madam, you will excuse me. I can do nothing for you."

Afterward, in speaking of this incident, President Lincoln said that the lady, as a representative of her class in Alexandria, reminded him of the story of the young man who had an aged father and mother owning considerable property. The young man being an only son, and believing that the old people had outlived their usefulness, assassinated them both. He was accused, tried and convicted of the murder. When the judge came to pass sentence upon him, and called upon him to give any reason he might have why the sentence of death should not be passed upon him, he with great promptness replied that he hoped the court would be lenient upon him because he was a poor orphan!

"BAP." McNABB'S BOOSTER

It is true that Lincoln did not drink, never swore, was a stranger to smoking and lived a moral life generally, but he did like horse-racing and chicken fighting. New Salem, Illinois, where Lincoln was "clerking," was known the neighborhood around as a "fast" town, and the average young man made no very desperate resistance when tempted to join in the drinking and gambling bouts.

"Bap." McNabb was famous for his ability in both the raising and the purchase of roosters of prime fighting quality, and when his birds fought the attendance was large. It was because of the "flunking" of one of "Bap.'s" roosters that Lincoln was enabled to make a point when criticising McClellan's unreadiness and lack of energy.

One night there was a fight on the schedule, one of "Bap." McNabb's birds being a contestant. "Bap." brought a little red rooster, whose fighting qualities had been well advertised for days in advance, and much interest was manifested in the outcome. As the result of these contests was generally a quarrel, in which each man, charging foul play, seized his victim, they chose Lincoln umpire, relying not only on his fairness but his ability to enforce his decisions. Judge Herndon, in his "Abraham Lincoln," says of this notable event:

"I cannot improve on the description furnished me in February, 1865, by one who was present.

"They formed a ring, and the time having arrived, Lincoln, with one hand on each hip and in a squatting position, cried, 'Ready.' Into the ring they toss their fowls, 'Bap.'s' red rooster along with the rest. But no sooner had the little beauty discovered what was to be done than he dropped his tail and ran.

"The crowd cheered, while 'Bap.,' in disappointment, picked him up and started away, losing his quarter (entrance fee) and carrying home his dishonored fowl. Once arrived at the latter place he threw his pet down with a feeling of indignation and chagrin.

"The little fellow, out of sight of all rivals, mounted a woodpile and proudly flirting out his feathers, crowed with all his might. 'Bap.' looked on in disgust.

"'Yes, you little cuss,' he exclaimed, irreverently, 'you're great on dress parade, but not worth a darn in a fight.'"

It is said, according to Judge Herndon, that Lincoln considered McClellan as "great on dress parade," but not so much in a fight.

A LOW-DOWN TRICK

When Lincoln was a candidate of the Know Nothings for the State Legislature, the party was over-confident, and the Democrats pursued a stillhunt. Lincoln was defeated. He compared the situation to one of the camp-followers of General Taylor's army, who had secured a barrel of cider, erected a tent, and commenced selling it to the thirsty soldiers at twenty-five cents a drink, but he had sold but little before another sharp one set up a tent at his back, and tapped the barrel so as to flow on his side, and peddled out No. 1 cider at five cents a drink, of course, getting the latter's entire trade on the borrowed capital.

"The Democrats," said Mr. Lincoln, "had played Knownothing on a cheaper scale than had the real devotees of Sam, and had raked down his pile with his own cider!"

END FOR END

Judge H. W. Beckwith, of Danville, Ill., in his "Personal Recollections of Lincoln," tells a story which is a good example of Lincoln's way of condensing the law and the facts of an issue in a story: "A man, by vile words, first provoked and then made a bodily attack upon another. The latter, in defending himself, gave the other much the worst of the encounter. The aggressor, to get even, had the one who thrashed him tried in our Circuit Court on a charge of an assault and battery. Mr. Lincoln defended, and told the jury that his client was in the fix of a man who, in going along the highway with a pitchfork on his shoulder, was attacked by a fierce dog that ran out at him from a farmer's dooryard. In parrying off the brute with the fork, its prongs stuck into the brute and killed him.

"'What made you kill my dog?' said the farmer.

"'What made him try to bite me?'

"'But why did you not go at him with the other end of the pitchfork?'

"'Why did he not come after me with his other end?'

"At this Mr. Lincoln whirled about in his long arms an imaginary dog, and pushed its tail end toward the jury. This was the defensive plea of 'son assault demesne'--loosely, that 'the other fellow brought on the fight,'--quickly told, and in a way the dullest mind would grasp and retain."

LET SIX SKUNKS GO

The President had decided to select a new War Minister, and the Leading Republican Senators thought the occasion was opportune to change the whole seven Cabinet ministers. They, therefore, earnestly advised him to make a clean sweep, and select seven new men, and so restore the waning confidence of the country.

The President listened with patient courtesy, and when the Senators had concluded, he said, with a characteristic gleam of humor in his eye:

"Gentlemen, your request for a change of the whole Cabinet because I have made one change reminds me of a story I once heard in Illinois, of a farmer who was much troubled by skunks. His wife insisted on his trying to get rid of them.

"He loaded his shotgun one moonlight night and awaited developments. After some time the wife heard the shotgun go off, and in a few minutes the farmer entered the house.

"'What luck have you?' asked she.

"'I hid myself behind the wood-pile,' said the old man, 'with the shotgun pointed towards the hen roost, and before long there appeared not one skunk, but seven. I took aim, blazed away, killed one, and he raised such a fearful smell that I concluded it was best to let the other six go.'"

The Senators laughed and retired.

HOW HE GOT BLACKSTONE

The following story was told by Mr. Lincoln to Mr. A. J. Conant, the artist, who painted his portrait in Springfield in 1860:

"One day a man who was migrating to the West drove up in front of my store with a wagon which contained his family and household plunder. He asked me if I would buy an old barrel for which he had no room in his wagon, and which he said contained nothing of special value. I did not want it, but to oblige him I bought it, and paid him, I think, half a dollar for it. Without further examination, I put it away in the store and forgot all about it. Some time after, in overhauling things, I came upon the barrel, and, emptying it upon the floor to see what it contained, I found at the bottom of the rubbish a complete edition of Blackstone's Commentaries. I began to read those famous works, and I had plenty of time; for during the long summer days, when the farmers were busy with their crops, my customers were few and far between. The more I read"--this he said with unusual emphasis--"the more intensely interested I became. Never in my whole life was my mind so thoroughly absorbed. I read until I devoured them."

"I CAN STAND IT IF THEY CAN"

United States Senator Benjamin Wade, of Ohio, Henry Winter Davis, of Maryland, and Wendell Phillips were strongly opposed to President Lincoln's re-election, and Wade and Davis issued a manifesto. Phillips made several warm speeches against Lincoln and his policy.

When asked if he had read the manifesto or any of Phillips' speeches, the President replied:

"I have not seen them, nor do I care to see them. I have seen enough to satisfy me that I am a failure, not only in the opinion of the people in rebellion, but of many distinguished politicians of my own party. But time will show whether I am right or they are right, and I am content to abide its decision.

"I have enough to look after without giving much of my time to the consideration of the subject of who shall be my successor in office. The position is not an easy one; and the occupant, whoever he may be, for the next four years, will have little leisure to pluck a thorn or plant a rose in his own pathway."

It was urged that this opposition must be embarrassing to his Administration, as well as damaging to the party. He replied: "Yes, that is true; but our friends, Wade, Davis, Phillips, and others are hard to please. I am not capable of doing so. I cannot please them without wantonly violating not only my oath, but the most vital principles upon which our government was founded.

"As to those who, like Wade and the rest, see fit to depreciate my policy and cavil at my official acts, I shall not complain of them. I accord them the utmost freedom of speech and liberty of the press, but shall not change the policy I have adopted in the full belief that I am right.

"I feel on this subject as an old Illinois farmer once expressed himself while eating cheese. He was interrupted in the midst of his repast by the entrance of his son, who exclaimed, 'Hold on, dad! there's skippers in that cheese you're eating!'

"'Never mind, Tom,' said he, as he kept on munching his cheese, 'if they can stand it I can.'"

LINCOLN MISTAKEN FOR ONCE

President Lincoln was compelled to acknowledge that he made at least one mistake in "sizing up" men. One day a very dignified man called at the White House, and Lincoln's heart fell when his visitor approached. The latter was portly, his face was full of apparent anxiety, and Lincoln was willing to wager a year's salary that he represented some Society for the Easy and Speedy Repression of Rebellions.

The caller talked fluently, but at no time did he give advice or suggest a way to put down the Confederacy. He was full of humor, told a clever story or two, and was entirely self-possessed.

At length the President inquired, "You are a clergyman, are you not, sir?"

"Not by a jug full," returned the stranger heartily.

Grasping him by the hand Lincoln shook it until the visitor squirmed. "You must lunch with us. I am glad to see you. I was afraid you were a preacher."

"I went to the Chicago Convention," the caller said, "as a friend of Mr. Seward. I have watched you narrowly ever since your inauguration, and I called merely to pay my respects. What I want to say is this: I think you are doing everything for the good of the country that is in the power of man to do. You are on the right track. As one of your constituents I now say to you, do in future as you d-- please, and I will support you!"

This was spoken with tremendous effect.

"Why," said Mr. Lincoln in great astonishment, "I took you to be a preacher. I thought you had come here to tell me how to take Richmond," and he again grasped the hand of his strange visitor.

Accurate and penetrating as Mr. Lincoln's judgment was concerning men, for once he had been wholly mistaken. The scene was comical in the extreme. The two men stood gazing at each other. A smile broke from the lips of the solemn wag and rippled over the wide expanse of his homely face like sunlight overspreading a continent, and Mr. Lincoln was convulsed with laughter. He stayed to lunch.

FORGOT EVERYTHING HE KNEW

President Lincoln, while entertaining a few friends, is said to have related the following anecdote of a man who knew too much:

During the administration of President Jackson there was a singular young gentleman employed in the Public Post Office in Washington.

His name was G.; he was from Tennessee, the son of a widow, a neighbor of the President, on which account the old hero had a kind feeling for him, and always got him out of difficulties with some of the higher officials, to whom his singular interference was distasteful.

Among other things, it is said of him that while employed in the General Post Office, on one occasion he had to copy a letter to Major H., a high official, in answer to an application made by an old gentleman in Virginia or Pennsylvania, for the establishment of a new post office.

The writer of the letter said the application could not be granted, in consequence of the applicant's "proximity" to another office.

When the letter came into G.'s hand to copy, being a great stickler for plainness, he altered "proximity" to "nearness to."

Major H. observed it, and asked G. why he altered his letter.

"Why," replied G., "because I don't think the man would understand what you mean by proximity."

"Well," said Major H., "try him; put in the 'proximity' again."

In a few days a letter was received from the applicant, in which he very indignantly said that his father had fought for liberty in the second war for independence, and he should like to have the name of the scoundrel who brought the charge of proximity or anything else wrong against him.

"There," said G., "did I not say so?"

G. carried his improvements so far that Mr. Berry, the Postmaster-General, said to him: "I don't want you any longer; you know too much."

Poor G. went out, but his old friend got him another place.

This time G.'s ideas underwent a change. He was one day very busy writing, when a stranger called in and asked him where the Patent Office was.

"I don't know," said G.

"Can you tell me where the Treasury Department is?" said the stranger.

"No," said G.

"Nor the President's house?"

"No."

The stranger finally asked him if he knew where the Capitol was.

"No," replied G.

"Do you live in Washington, sir."

"Yes, sir," said G.

"Good Lord! and don't you know where the Patent Office, Treasury, President's House and Capitol are?"

"Stranger," said G., "I was turned out of the post office for knowing too much. I don't mean to offend in that way again.

"I am paid for keeping this book.

"I believe I know that much; but if you find me knowing anything more you may take my head."

"Good morning," said the stranger.

HE LOVED A GOOD STORY

Judge Breese, of the Supreme bench, one of the most distinguished of American jurists, and a man of great personal dignity, was about to open court at Springfield, when Lincoln called out in his hearty way: "Hold on, Breese! Don't open court yet! Here's Bob Blackwell just going to tell a story!" The judge passed on without replying, evidently regarding it as beneath the dignity of the Supreme Court to delay proceedings for the sake of a story.

HEELS RAN AWAY WITH THEM

In an argument against the opposite political party at one time during a campaign, Lincoln said: "My opponent uses a figurative expression to the effect that 'the Democrats are vulnerable in the heel, but they are sound in the heart and head.' The first branch of the figure--that is the Democrats are vulnerable in the heel--I admit is not merely figuratively but literally true. Who that looks but for a moment at their hundreds of officials scampering away with the public money to Texas, to Europe, and to every spot of the earth where a villain may hope to find refuge from justice, can at all doubt that they are most distressingly affected in their heels with a species of running itch?

"It seems that this malady of their heels operates on the sound-headed and honest-hearted creatures very much as the cork leg in the comic song did on its owner, which, when he once got started on it, the more he tried to stop it, the more it would run away.

"At the hazard of wearing this point threadbare, I will relate an anecdote the situation calls to my mind, which seems to be too strikingly in point to be omitted. A witty Irish soldier, who was always boasting of his bravery when no danger was near, but who invariably retreated without orders at the first charge of the engagement, being asked by his captain why he did so, replied, 'Captain, I have as brave a heart as Julius Caesar ever had, but somehow or other, whenever danger approaches, my cowardly legs will run away with it.'

"So with the opposite party--they take the public money into their hands for the most laudable purpose that wise heads and honest hearts can dictate; but before they can possibly get it out again, their rascally, vulnerable heels will run away with them."

WANTED TO BURN HIM DOWN TO THE STUMP

Preston King once introduced A. J. Bleeker to the President, and the latter, being an applicant for office, was about to hand Mr. Lincoln his vouchers, when he was asked to read them. Bleeker had not read very far when the President disconcerted him by the exclamation, "Stop a minute! You remind me exactly of the man who killed the dog; in fact, you are just like him."

"In what respect?" asked Bleeker, not feeling he had received a compliment.

"Well," replied the President, "this man had made up his mind to kill his dog, an ugly brute, and proceeded to knock out his brains with a club. He continued striking the dog after the latter was dead until a friend protested, exclaiming, 'You needn't strike him any more; the dog is dead; you killed him at the first blow.'

"'Oh, yes,' said he, 'I know that; but I believe in punishment after death.' So, I see, you do."

Bleeker acknowledged it was possible to overdo a good thing, and then came back at the President with an anecdote of a good priest who converted an Indian from heathenism to Christianity; the only difficulty he had with him was to get him to pray for his enemies. "This Indian had been taught to overcome and destroy all his friends he didn't like," said Bleeker, "but the priest told him that while that might be the Indian method, it was not the doctrine of Christianity or the Bible. 'Saint Paul distinctly says,' the priest told him, 'If thine enemy hunger, feed him; if he thirst, give him drink.'

"The Indian shook his head at this, but when the priest added, 'For in so doing thou shalt heap coals of fire on his head,' Poor Lo was overcome with emotion, fell on his knees, and with outstretched hands and uplifted eyes invoked all sorts of blessings on the heads of all his enemies, supplicating for pleasant hunting-grounds, a large supply of squaws, lots of papooses, and all other Indian comforts.

"Finally the good priest interrupted him (as you did me, Mr. President), exclaiming, 'Stop, my son! You have discharged your Christian duty, and have done more than enough.'

"'Oh, no, father,' replied the Indian; 'let me pray! I want to burn him down to the stump!'"

HAD A "KICK" COMING

During the war, one of the Northern Governors, who was able, earnest and untiring in aiding the administration, but always complaining, sent dispatch after dispatch to the War Office, protesting against the methods used in raising troops. After reading all his papers, the President said, in a cheerful and reassuring tone to the Adjutant-General:

"Never mind, never mind; those dispatches don't mean anything. Just go right ahead. The Governor is like a boy I once saw at a launching. When everything was ready, they picked out a boy and sent him under the ship to knock away the trigger and let her go.

"At the critical moment everything depended on the boy. He had to do the job well by a direct, vigorous blow, and then lie flat and keep still while the boat slid over him.

"The boy did everything right, but he yelled as if he were being murdered from the time he got under the keel until he got out. I thought the hide was all scraped off his back, but he wasn't hurt at all.

"The master of the yard told me that this boy was always chosen for that job; that he did his work well; that he never had been hurt, but that he always squealed in that way.

"That's just the way with Governor --. Make up your mind that he is not hurt, and that he is doing the work right, and pay no attention to his squealing. He only wants to make you understand how hard his task is, and that he is on hand performing it."

THE CASE OF BETSY ANN DOUGHERTY

Many requests and petitions made to Mr. Lincoln when he was President were ludicrous and trifling, but he always entered into them with that humor-loving spirit that was such a relief from the grave duties of his great office.

Once a party of Southerners called on him in behalf of one Betsy Ann Dougherty. The spokesman, who was an ex-Governor, said:

"Mr. President, Betsy Ann Dougherty is a good woman. She lived in my county and did my washing for a long time. Her husband went off and joined the rebel army, and I wish you would give her a protection paper." The solemnity of this appeal struck Mr. Lincoln as uncommonly ridiculous.

The two men looked at each other--the Governor desperately earnest, and the President masking his humor behind the gravest exterior. At last Mr. Lincoln asked, with inimitable gravity, "Was Betsy Ann a good washerwoman?" "Oh, yes, sir, she was, indeed."

"Was your Betsy Ann an obliging woman?" "Yes, she was certainly very kind," responded the Governor, soberly. "Could she do other things than wash?" continued Mr. Lincoln with the same portentous gravity.

"Oh, yes; she was very kind--very."

"Where is Betsy Ann?"

"She is now in New York, and wants to come back to Missouri, but she is afraid of banishment."

"Is anybody meddling with her?"

"No; but she is afraid to come back unless you will give her a protection paper."

Thereupon Mr. Lincoln wrote on a visiting card the following:

"Let Betsy Ann Dougherty alone as long as she behaves herself."

"A. LINCOLN."

He handed this card to her advocate, saying, "Give this to Betsy Ann."

"But, Mr. President, couldn't you write a few words to the officers that would insure her protection?"

"No," said Mr. Lincoln, "officers have no time now to read letters. Tell Betsy Ann to put a string in this card and hang it around her neck. When the officers see this, they will keep their hands off your Betsy Ann."

HAD TO WEAR A WOODEN SWORD

Captain "Abe" Lincoln and his company (in the Black Hawk War) were without any sort of military knowledge, and both were forced to acquire such knowledge by attempts at drilling. Which was the more awkward, the "squad" or the commander, it would have been difficult to decide.

In one of Lincoln's earliest military problems was involved the process of getting his company "endwise" through a gate. Finally he shouted, "This company is dismissed for two minutes, when it will fall in again on the other side of the gate!"

Lincoln was one of the first of his company to be arraigned for unmilitary conduct. Contrary to the rules he fired a gun "within the limits," and had his sword taken from him. The next infringement of rules was by some of the men, who stole a quantity of liquor, drank it, and became unfit for duty, straggling out of the ranks the next day, and not getting together again until late at night.

For allowing this lawlessness the captain was condemned to wear a wooden sword for two days. These were merely interesting but trivial incidents of the campaign. Lincoln was from the very first popular with his men, although one of them told him to "go to the devil."

GETTING RID OF AN ELEPHANT

Charles A. Dana, who was Assistant Secretary of War under Mr. Stanton, relates the following: A certain Thompson had been giving the government considerable trouble. Dana received information that Thompson was about to escape to Liverpool.

Calling upon Stanton, Dana was referred to Mr. Lincoln.

"The President was at the White House, business hours were over, Lincoln was washing his hands. 'Hallo, Dana,' said he, as I opened the door, 'what is it now?' 'Well, sir,' I said, 'here is the Provost Marshal of Portland, who reports that Jacob Thompson is to be in town to-night, and inquires what orders we have to give.' 'What does Stanton say?' he asked. 'Arrest him,' I replied. 'Well,' he continued, drawling his words, 'I rather guess not. When you have an elephant on your hands, and he wants to run away, better let him run.'"

CHARACTERISTIC OF LINCOLN

One man who knew Lincoln at New Salem, says the first time he saw him he was lying on a trundle-bed covered with books and papers and rocking a cradle with his foot.

The whole scene was entirely characteristic--Lincoln reading and studying, and at the same time helping his landlady by quieting her child.

A gentleman who knew Mr. Lincoln well in early manhood says: "Lincoln at this period had nothing but plenty of friends."

After the customary hand-shaking on one occasion in the White House at Washington several gentlemen came forward and asked the President for his autograph. One of them gave his name as "Cruikshank." "That reminds me," said Mr. Lincoln, "of what I used to be called when a young man--'Long-shanks!'"

"PLOUGH ALL 'ROUND HIM"

Governor Blank went to the War Department one day in a towering rage:

"I suppose you found it necessary to make large concessions to him, as he returned from you perfectly satisfied," suggested a friend.

"Oh, no," the President replied, "I did not concede anything. You have heard how that Illinois farmer got rid of a big log that was too big to haul out, too knotty to split, and too wet and soggy to burn.

"'Well, now,' said he, in response to the inquiries of his neighbors one Sunday, as to how he got rid of it, 'well, now, boys, if you won't divulge the secret, I'll tell you how I got rid of it--I ploughed around it.'

"Now," remarked Lincoln, in conclusion, "don't tell anybody, but that's the way I got rid of Governor Blank. I ploughed all round him, but it took me three mortal hours to do it, and I was afraid every minute he'd see what I was at."

LOST HIS CERTIFICATE OF CHARACTER

Mr. Lincoln prepared his first inaugural address in a room over a store in Springfield. His only reference works were Henry Clay's great compromise speech of 1850, Andrew Jackson's Proclamation against Nullification, Webster's great reply to Hayne, and a copy of the Constitution.

When Mr. Lincoln started for Washington, to be inaugurated, the inaugural address was placed in a special satchel and guarded with special care. At Harrisburg the satchel was given in charge of Robert T. Lincoln, who accompanied his father. Before the train started from Harrisburg the precious satchel was missing. Robert thought he had given it to a waiter at the hotel, but a long search failed to reveal the missing satchel with its precious document. Lincoln was annoyed, angry, and finally in despair. He felt certain that the address was lost beyond recovery, and, as it only lacked ten days until the inauguration, he had no time to prepare another. He had not even preserved the notes from which the original copy had been written.

Mr. Lincoln went to Ward Lamon, his former law partner, then one of his bodyguards, and informed him of the loss in the following words:

"Lamon, I guess I have lost my certificate of moral character, written by myself. Bob has lost my gripsack containing my inaugural address." Of course, the misfortune reminded him of a story.

"I feel," said Mr. Lincoln, "a good deal as the old member of the Methodist Church did when he lost his wife at the camp meeting, and went up to an old elder of the church and asked him if he could tell him whereabouts in h--l his wife was. In fact, I am in a worse fix than my Methodist friend, for if it were only a wife that were missing, mine would be sure to bob up somewhere."

The clerk at the hotel told Mr. Lincoln that he would probably find his missing satchel in the baggage-room. Arriving there, Mr. Lincoln saw a satchel which he thought was his, and it was passed out to him. His key fitted the lock, but alas! when it was opened the satchel contained only a soiled shirt, some paper collars, a pack of cards and a bottle of whisky. A few minutes later the satchel containing the inaugural address was found among the pile of baggage.

The recovery of the address also reminded Mr. Lincoln of a story, which is thus narrated by Ward Lamon in his "Recollections of Abraham Lincoln"

The loss of the address and the search for it was the subject of a great deal of amusement. Mr. Lincoln said many funny things in connection with the incident. One of them was that he knew a fellow once who had saved up fifteen hundred dollars, and had placed it in a private banking establishment. The bank soon failed, and he afterward received ten per cent of his investment. He then took his one hundred and fifty dollars and deposited it in a savings bank, where he was sure it would be safe. In a short time this bank also failed, and he received at the final settlement ten per cent on the amount deposited. When the fifteen dollars was paid over to him, he held it in his hand and looked at it thoughtfully; then he said, "Now, darn you, I have got you reduced to a portable shape, so I'll put you in my pocket." Suiting the action to the word, Mr. Lincoln took his address from the bag and carefully placed it in the inside pocket of his vest, but held on to the satchel with as much interest as if it still contained his "certificate of moral character."

NOTE PRESENTED FOR PAYMENT

The great English funny paper, London "Punch," printed this cartoon on September 27th, 1862. It is intended to convey the idea that Lincoln, having asserted that the war would be over in ninety days, had not redeemed his word: The text under the Cartoon in Punch was:

DOG WAS A "LEETLE BIT AHEAD."

Lincoln could not sympathize with those Union generals who were prone to indulge in high-sounding promises, but whose performances did not by any means come up to their predictions as to what they would do if they ever met the enemy face to face. He said one day, just after one of these braggarts had been soundly thrashed by the Confederates:

"These fellows remind me of the fellow who owned a dog which, so he said, just hungered and thirsted to combat and eat up wolves. It was a difficult matter, so the owner declared, to keep that dog from devoting the entire twenty-four hours of each day to the destruction of his enemies. He just 'hankered' to get at them.

"One day a party of this dog-owner's friends thought to have some sport. These friends heartily disliked wolves, and were anxious to see the dog eat up a few thousand. So they organized a hunting party and invited the dog-owner and the dog to go with them. They desired to be personally present when the wolf-killing was in progress.

"It was noticed that the dog-owner was not over-enthusiastic in the matter; he pleaded a 'business engagement,' but as he was the most notorious and torpid of the town loafers, and wouldn't have recognized a 'business engagement' had he met it face to face, his excuse was treated with contempt. Therefore he had to go.

"The dog, however, was glad enough to go, and so the party started out. Wolves were in plenty, and soon a pack was discovered, but when the 'wolf-hound' saw the ferocious animals he lost heart, and, putting his tail between his legs, endeavored to slink away. At last--after many trials--he was enticed into the small growth of underbrush where the wolves had secreted themselves, and yelps of terror betrayed the fact that the battle was on.

"Away flew the wolves, the dog among them, the hunting party following on horseback. The wolves seemed frightened, and the dog was restored to public favor. It really looked as if he had the savage creatures on the run, as he was fighting heroically when last sighted.

"Wolves and dog soon disappeared, and it was not until the party arrived at a distant farmhouse that news of the combatants was gleaned.

'Have you seen anything of a wolf-dog and a pack of wolves around here?' was the question anxiously put to the male occupant of the house, who stood idly leaning upon the gate.

"'Yep,' was the short answer.

"'How were they going?'

"'Purty fast.'

"'What was their position when you saw them?'

"'Well,' replied the farmer, in a most exasperatingly deliberate way, 'the dog was a leetle bit ahead.'

"Now, gentlemen," concluded the President, "that's the position in which you'll find most of these bragging generals when they get into a fight with the enemy. That's why I don't like military orators."

NOISE LIKE A TURNIP.

"Every man has his own peculiar and particular way of getting at and doing things," said President Lincoln one day, "and he is often criticized because that way is not the one adopted by others. The great idea is to accomplish what you set out to do. When a man is successful in whatever he attempts, he has many imitators, and the methods used are not so closely scrutinized, although no man who is of good intent will resort to mean, underhanded, scurvy tricks.

"That reminds me of a fellow out in Illinois, who had better luck in getting prairie chickens than any one in the neighborhood. He had a rusty old gun no other man dared to handle; he never seemed to exert himself, being listless and indifferent when out after game, but he always brought home all the chickens he could carry, while some of the others, with their finely trained dogs and latest improved fowling-pieces, came home alone.

"'How is it, Jake?' inquired one sportsman, who, although a good shot, and knew something about hunting, was often unfortunate, 'that you never come home without a lot of birds?'

"Jake grinned, half closed his eyes, and replied: 'Oh, I don't know that there's anything queer about it. I jes' go ahead an' git 'em.'

"'Yes, I know you do; but how do you do it?'

"'You'll tell.'

"'Honest, Jake, I won't say a word. Hope to drop dead this minute.'

"'Never say nothing, if I tell you?'

"'Cross my heart three times.'

"This reassured Jake, who put his mouth close to the ear of his eager questioner, and said, in a whisper:

"'All you got to do is jes' to hide in a fence corner an' make a noise like a turnip. That'll bring the chickens every time.'"

WARDING OFF GOD'S VENGEANCE

When Lincoln was a candidate for re-election to the Illinois Legislature in 1836, a meeting was advertised to be held in the courthouse in Springfield, at which candidates of opposing parties were to speak. This gave men of spirit and capacity a fine opportunity to show the stuff of which they were made.

George Forquer was one of the most prominent citizens; he had been a Whig, but became a Democrat--possibly for the reason that by means of the change he secured the position of Government land register, from President Andrew Jackson. He had the largest and finest house in the city, and there was a new and striking appendage to it, called a lightning-rod! The meeting was very large. Seven Whig and seven Democratic candidates spoke.

Lincoln closed the discussion. A Kentuckian (Joshua F. Speed), who had heard Henry Clay and other distinguished Kentucky orators, stood near Lincoln, and stated afterward that he "never heard a more effective speaker; . . . the crowd seemed to be swayed by him as he pleased." What occurred during the closing portion of this meeting must be given in full, from Judge Arnold's book:

"Forquer, although not a candidate, asked to be heard for the Democrats, in reply to Lincoln. He was a good speaker, and well known throughout the county. His special task that day was to attack and ridicule the young countryman from Salem.

"Turning to Lincoln, who stood within a few feet of him, he said: 'This young man must be taken down, and I am truly sorry that the task devolves upon me.' He then proceeded, in a very overbearing way, and with an assumption of great superiority, to attack Lincoln and his speech. He was fluent and ready with the rough sarcasm of the stump, and he went on to ridicule the person, dress and arguments of Lincoln with so much success that Lincoln's friends feared that he would be embarrassed and overthrown."

The Clary's Grove boys were present, and were restrained with difficulty from "getting up a fight" in behalf of their favorite (Lincoln), they and all his friends feeling that the attack was ungenerous and unmanly.)

"Lincoln, however, stood calm, but his flashing eye and pale cheek indicated his indignation. As soon as Forquer had closed he took the stand, and first answered his opponent's arguments fully and triumphantly. So impressive were his words and manner that a hearer (Joshua F. Speed) believes that he can remember to this day and repeat some of the expressions.

"Among other things he said: 'The gentleman commenced his speech by saying that "this young man," alluding to me, "must be taken down." I am not so young in years as I am in the tricks and the trades of a politician, but,' said he, pointing to Forquer, 'live long or die young, I would rather die now than, like the gentleman, change my politics, and with the change receive an office worth $3,000 a year, and then,' continued he, 'feel obliged to erect a lightning-rod over my house, to protect a guilty conscience from an offended God!'"

JEFF DAVIS AND CHARLES THE FIRST

Jefferson Davis insisted on being recognized by his official title as commander or President in the regular negotiation with the Government. This Mr. Lincoln would not consent to.

Mr. Hunter thereupon referred to the correspondence between King Charles the First and his Parliament as a precedent for a negotiation between a constitutional ruler and rebels. Mr. Lincoln's face then wore that indescribable expression which generally preceded his hardest hits, and he remarked: "Upon questions of history, I must refer you to Mr. Seward, for he is posted in such things, and I don't profess to be; but my only distinct recollection of the matter is, that Charles lost his head."

LOVED SOLDIERS' HUMOR

Lincoln loved anything that savored of wit or humor among the soldiers. He used to relate two stories to show, he said, that neither death nor danger could quench the grim humor of the American soldier:

"A soldier of the Army of the Potomac was being carried to the rear of battle with both legs shot off, who, seeing a pie-woman, called out, 'Say, old lady, are them pies sewed or pegged?'

"And there was another one of the soldiers at the battle of Chancellorsville, whose regiment, waiting to be called into the fight, was taking coffee. The hero of the story put to his lips a crockery mug which he had carried with care through several campaigns. A stray bullet, just missing the tinker's head, dashed the mug into fragments and left only the handle on his finger. Turning his head in that direction, he scowled, 'Johnny, you can't do that again!'"

BAD TIME FOR A BARBECUE

Captain T. W. S. Kidd of Springfield was the crier of the court in the days when Mr. Lincoln used to ride the circuit.

"I was younger than he," says Captain Kidd, "but he had a sort of admiration for me, and never failed to get me into his stories. I was a story-teller myself in those days, and he used to laugh very heartily at some of the stories I told him.

"Now and then he got me into a good deal of trouble. I was a Democrat, and was in politics more or less. A good many of our Democratic voters at that time were Irishmen. They came to Illinois in the days of the old canal, and did their honest share in making that piece of internal improvement an accomplished fact.

"One time Mr. Lincoln told the story of one of those important young fellows--not an Irishman--who lived in every town, and have the cares of state on their shoulders. This young fellow met an Irishman on the street, and called to him, officiously: 'Oh, Mike, I'm awful glad I met you. We've got to do something to wake up the boys. The campaign is coming on, and we've got to get out voters. We've just had a meeting up here, and we're going to have the biggest barbecue that ever was heard of in Illinois. We are going to roast two whole oxen, and we're going to have Douglas and Governor Cass and some one from Kentucky, and all the big Democratic guns, and we're going to have a great big time.'

"'By dad, that's good!' says the Irishman. 'The byes need stirrin' up.'

"'Yes, and you're on one of the committees, and you want to hustle around and get them waked up, Mike.'

"'When is the barbecue to be?' asked Mike.

"'Friday, two weeks.'

"'Friday, is it? Well, I'll make a nice committeeman, settin' the barbecue on a day with half of the Dimocratic party of Sangamon county can't ate a bite of mate. Go on wid ye.'

"Lincoln told that story in one of his political speeches, and when the laugh was over he said: 'Now, gentlemen, I know that story is true, for Tom Kidd told it to me.' And then the Democrats would make trouble for me for a week afterward, and I'd have to explain."

HE'D SEE IT AGAIN

About two years before Lincoln was nominated for the Presidency he went to Bloomington, Illinois, to try a case of some importance. His opponent--who afterward reached a high place in his profession--was a young man of ability, sensible but sensitive, and one to whom the loss of a case was a great blow. He therefore studied hard and made much preparation.

This particular case was submitted to the jury late at night, and, although anticipating a favorable verdict, the young attorney spent a sleepless night in anxiety. Early next morning he learned, to his great chagrin, that he had lost the case.

Lincoln met him at the court-house some time after the jury had come in, and asked him what had become of his case.

With lugubrious countenance and in a melancholy tone the young man replied, "It's gone to hell."

"Oh, well," replied Lincoln, "then you will see it again."

CALL ANOTHER WITNESS

When arguing a case in court, Mr. Lincoln never used a word which the dullest juryman could not understand. Rarely, if ever, did a Latin term creep into his arguments. A lawyer, quoting a legal maxim one day in court, turned to Lincoln, and said: "That is so, is it not, Mr. Lincoln?"

"If that's Latin." Lincoln replied, "you had better call another witness."

A CONTEST WITH LITTLE "TAD"

Mr. Carpenter, the artist, relates the following incident: "Some photographers came up to the White House to make some stereoscopic studies for me of the President's office. They requested a dark closet in which to develop the pictures, and, without a thought that I was infringing upon anybody's rights, I took them to an unoccupied room of which little 'Tad' had taken possession a few days before, and, with the aid of a couple of servants, had fitted up a miniature theater, with stage, curtains, orchestra, stalls, parquette and all. Knowing that the use required would interfere with none of his arrangements, I led the way to this apartment.

"Everything went on well, and one or two pictures had been taken, when suddenly there was an uproar. The operator came back to the office and said that 'Tad' had taken great offense at the occupation of his room without his consent, and had locked the door, refusing all admission.

"The chemicals had been taken inside, and there was no way of getting at them, he having carried off the key. In the midst of this conversation 'Tad' burst in, in a fearful passion. He laid all the blame upon me--said that I had no right to use his room, and the men should not go in even to get their things. He had locked the door and they should not go there again--'they had no business in his room!'

"Mr. Lincoln was sitting for a photograph, and was still in the chair. He said, very mildly, 'Tad, go and unlock the door.' Tad went off muttering into his mother's room, refusing to obey. I followed him into the passage, but no coaxing would pacify him. Upon my return to the President, I found him still patiently in the chair, from which he had not risen. He said: 'Has not the boy opened the door?' I replied that we could do nothing with him--he had gone off in a great pet. Mr. Lincoln's lips came together firmly, and then, suddenly rising, he strode across the passage with the air of one bent on punishment, and disappeared in the domestic apartments. Directly he returned with the key to the theater, which he unlocked himself.

"'Tad,' said he, half apologetically, 'is a peculiar child. He was violently excited when I went to him. I said, "Tad, do you know that you are making your father a great deal of trouble?" He burst into tears, instantly giving me up the key.'"

REMINDED HIM OF "A LITTLE STORY"

When Lincoln's attention was called to the fact that, at one time in his boyhood, he had spelled the name of the Deity with a small "g," he replied:

"That reminds me of a little story. It came about that a lot of Confederate mail was captured by the Union forces, and, while it was not exactly the proper thing to do, some of our soldiers opened several letters written by the Southerners at the front to their people at home.

"In one of these missives the writer, in a postscript, jotted down this assertion

"'We'll lick the Yanks termorrer, if goddlemity (God Almighty) spares our lives.'

"That fellow was in earnest, too, as the letter was written the day before the second battle of Manassas."

"FETCHED SEVERAL SHORT ONES"

"The first time I ever remember seeing 'Abe' Lincoln," is the testimony of one of his neighbors, "was when I was a small boy and had gone with my father to attend some kind of an election. One of the neighbors, James Larkins, was there.

"Larkins was a great hand to brag on anything he owned. This time it was his horse. He stepped up before 'Abe,' who was in a crowd, and commenced talking to him, boasting all the while of his animal.

"'I have got the best horse in the country,' he shouted to his young listener. 'I ran him nine miles in exactly three minutes, and he never fetched a long breath.'

"'I presume,' said 'Abe,' rather dryly, 'he fetched a good many short ones, though.'"

McCLELLAN WAS "INTRENCHING"

About a week after the Chicago Convention, a gentleman from New York called upon the President, in company with the Assistant Secretary of War, Mr. Dana.

In the course of conversation, the gentleman said: "What do you think, Mr. President, is the reason General McClellan does not reply to the letter from the Chicago Convention?"

"Oh!" replied Mr. Lincoln, with a characteristic twinkle of the eye, "he is intrenching!"

MAKE SOMETHING OUT OF IT, ANYWAY

From the day of his nomination by the Chicago convention, gifts poured in upon Lincoln. Many of these came in the form of wearing apparel. Mr. George Lincoln, of Brooklyn, who brought to Springfield, in January, 1861, a handsome silk hat to the President-elect, the gift of a New York hatter, told some friends that in receiving the hat Lincoln laughed heartily over the gifts of clothing, and remarked to Mrs. Lincoln: "Well, wife, if nothing else comes out of this scrape, we are going to have some new clothes, are we not?"

VICIOUS OXEN HAVE SHORT HORNS

In speaking of the many mean and petty acts of certain members of Congress, the President, while talking on the subject one day with friends, said:

"I have great sympathy for these men, because of their temper and their weakness; but I am thankful that the good Lord has given to the vicious ox short horns, for if their physical courage were equal to their vicious disposition, some of us in this neck of the woods would get hurt."

LINCOLN'S NAME FOR "WEEPING WATER"

"I was speaking one time to Mr. Lincoln," said Governor Saunders, of Nebraska, of a little Nebraskan settlement on the Weeping Water, a stream in our State."

"'Weeping Water!' said he.

"Then with a twinkle in his eye, he continued.

"'I suppose the Indians out there call Minneboohoo, don't they? They ought to, if Laughing Water is Minnehaha in their language.'"

PETER CARTWRIGHT'S DESCRIPTION OF LINCOLN

Peter Cartwright, the famous and eccentric old Methodist preacher, who used to ride a church circuit, as Mr. Lincoln and others did the court circuit, did not like Lincoln very well, probably because Mr. Lincoln was not a member of his flock, and once defeated the preacher for Congress. This was Cartwright's description of Lincoln: "This Lincoln is a man six feet four inches tall, but so angular that if you should drop a plummet from the center of his head it would cut him three times before it touched his feet."

NO DEATHS IN HIS HOUSE

A gentleman was relating to the President how a friend of his had been driven away from New Orleans as a Unionist, and how, on his expulsion, when he asked to see the writ by which he was expelled, the deputation which called on him told him the Government would do nothing illegal, and so they had issued no illegal writs, and simply meant to make him go of his own free will.

"Well," said Mr. Lincoln, "that reminds me of a hotel-keeper down at St. Louis, who boasted that he never had a death in his hotel, for whenever a guest was dying in his house he carried him out to die in the gutter."

PAINTED HIS PRINCIPLES

The day following the adjournment of the Baltimore Convention, at which President Lincoln was re-nominated, various political organizations called to pay their respects to the President. While the Philadelphia delegation was being presented, the chairman of that body, in introducing one of the members, said:

"Mr. President, this is Mr. S., of the second district of our State,--a most active and earnest friend of yours and the cause. He has, among other things, been good enough to paint, and present to our league rooms, a most beautiful portrait of yourself."

President Lincoln took the gentleman's hand in his, and shaking it cordially said, with a merry voice, "I presume, sir, in painting your beautiful portrait, you took your idea of me from my principles and not from my person."

DIGNIFYING THE STATUTE

Lincoln was married--he balked at the first date set for the ceremony and did not show up at all--November 4, 1842, under most happy auspices. The officiating clergyman, the Rev. Mr. Dresser, used the Episcopal church service for marriage. Lincoln placed the ring upon the bride's finger, and said, "With this ring I now thee wed, and with all my worldly goods I thee endow."

Judge Thomas C. Browne, who was present, exclaimed, "Good gracious, Lincoln! the statute fixes all that!"

"Oh, well," drawled Lincoln, "I just thought I'd add a little dignity to the statute."

GIVING AWAY THE CASE

Between the first election and inauguration of Mr. Lincoln the disunion sentiment grew rapidly in the South, and President Buchanan's failure to stop the open acts of secession grieved Mr. Lincoln sorely. Mr. Lincoln had a long talk with his friend, Judge Gillespie, over the state of affairs. One incident of the conversation is thus narrated by the Judge:

"When I retired, it was the master of the house and chosen ruler of the country who saw me to my room. 'Joe,' he said, as he was about to leave me, 'I am reminded and I suppose you will never forget that trial down in Montgomery county, where the lawyer associated with you gave away the whole case in his opening speech. I saw you signaling to him, but you couldn't stop him.

"'Now, that's just the way with me and Buchanan. He is giving away the case, and I have nothing to say, and can't stop him. Good-night.'"

POSING WITH A BROOMSTICK

Mr. Leonard Volk, the artist, relates that, being in Springfield when Lincoln's nomination for President was announced, he called upon Mr. Lincoln, whom he found looking smiling and happy. "I exclaimed, 'I am the first man from Chicago, I believe, who has had the honor of congratulating you on your nomination for President.' Then those two great hands took both of mine with a grasp never to be forgotten, and while shaking, I said, 'Now that you will doubtless be the next President of the United States, I want to make a statue of you, and shall try my best to do you justice.'

"Said he, 'I don't doubt it, for I have come to the conclusion that you are an honest man,' and with that greeting, I thought my hands in a fair way of being crushed.

"On the Sunday following, by agreement, I called to make a cast of Mr. Lincoln's hands. I asked him to hold something in his hands, and told him a stick would do. Thereupon he went to the woodshed, and I heard the saw go, and he soon returned to the dining-room, whittling off the end of a piece of broom handle. I remarked to him that he need not whittle off the edges. 'Oh, well,' said he, 'I thought I would like to have it nice.'"

"BOTH LENGTH AND BREADTH"

During Lincoln's first and only term in Congress--he was elected in 1846--he formed quite a cordial friendship with Stephen A. Douglas, a member of the United States Senate from Illinois, and the beaten one in the contest as to who should secure the hand of Miss Mary Todd. Lincoln was the winner; Douglas afterwards beat him for the United States Senate, but Lincoln went to the White House.

During all of the time that they were rivals in love and in politics they remained the best of friends personally. They were always glad to see each other, and were frequently together. The disparity in their size was always the more noticeable upon such occasions, and they well deserved their nicknames of "Long Abe" and the "Little Giant." Lincoln was the tallest man in the National House of Representatives, and Douglas the shortest (and perhaps broadest) man the Senate, and when they appeared on the streets together much merriment was created. Lincoln, when joked about the matter, replied, in a very serious tone, "Yes, that's about the length and breadth of it."

"ABE" RECITES A SONG

Lincoln couldn't sing, and he also lacked the faculty of musical adaptation. He had a liking for certain ballads and songs, and while he memorized and recited their lines, someone else did the singing. Lincoln often recited for the delectation of his friends, the following, the authorship of which is unknown:

The first factional fight in old Ireland, they say, Was all on account of St. Patrick's birthday; It was somewhere about midnight without any doubt, And certain it is, it made a great rout.

On the eighth day of March, as some people say, St. Patrick at midnight he first saw the day; While others assert 'twas the ninth he was born-- 'Twas all a mistake--between midnight and morn.

Some blamed the baby, some blamed the clock; Some blamed the doctor, some the crowing cock. With all these close questions sure no one could know, Whether the babe was too fast or the clock was too slow.

Some fought for the eighth, for the ninth some would die; He who wouldn't see right would have a black eye. At length these two factions so positive grew, They each had a birthday, and Pat he had two.

Till Father Mulcahay who showed them their sins, He said none could have two birthdays but as twins. "Now boys, don't be fighting for the eight or the nine; Don't quarrel so always, now why not combine."

Combine eight with nine. It is the mark; Let that be the birthday. Amen! said the clerk. So all got blind drunk, which completed their bliss, And they've kept up the practice from that day to this.

"MANAGE TO KEEP HOUSE"

Senator John Sherman, of Ohio, introduced his brother, William T. Sherman (then a civilian) to President Lincoln in March, 1861. Sherman had offered his services, but, as in the case of Grant, they had been refused.

After the Senator had transacted his business with the President, he said: "Mr. President, this is my brother, Colonel Sherman, who is just up from Louisiana; he may give you some information you want."

To this Lincoln replied, as reported by Senator Sherman himself: "Ah! How are they getting along down there?"

Sherman answered: "They think they are getting along swimmingly; they are prepared for war."

To which Lincoln responded: "Oh, well, I guess we'll manage to keep the house."

"Tecump," whose temper was not the mildest, broke out on "Brother John" as soon as they were out of the White House, cursed the politicians roundly, and wound up with, "You have got things in a h--l of a fix, and you may get out as best you can."

Sherman was one of the very few generals who gave Lincoln little or no worry.

GRANT "TUMBLED" RIGHT AWAY

General Grant told this story about Lincoln some years after the War:

"Just after receiving my commission as lieutenant-general the President called me aside to speak to me privately. After a brief reference to the military situation, he said he thought he could illustrate what he wanted to say by a story. Said he:

"'At one time there was a great war among the animals, and one side had great difficulty in getting a commander who had sufficient confidence in himself. Finally they found a monkey by the name of Jocko, who said he thought he could command their army if his tail could be made a little longer. So they got more tail and spliced it on to his caudal appendage.

"'He looked at it admiringly, and then said he thought he ought to have still more tail. This was added, and again he called for more. The splicing process was repeated many times until they had coiled Jocko's tail around the room, filling all the space.

"'Still he called for more tail, and, there being no other place to coil it, they began wrapping it around his shoulders. He continued his call for more, and they kept on winding the additional tail around him until its weight broke him down.'

"I saw the point, and, rising from my chair, replied, 'Mr. President, I will not call for any more assistance unless I find it impossible to do with what I already have.'"

"DON'T KILL HIM WITH YOUR FIST"

Ward Lamon, Marshal of the District of Columbia during Lincoln's time in Washington, was a powerful man; his strength was phenomenal, and a blow from his fist was like unto that coming from the business end of a sledge.

Lamon tells this story, the hero of which is not mentioned by name, but in all probability his identity can be guessed:

"On one occasion, when the fears of the loyal element of the city (Washington) were excited to fever-heat, a free fight near the old National Theatre occurred about eleven o'clock one night. An officer, in passing the place, observed what was going on, and seeing the great number of persons engaged, he felt it to be his duty to command the peace.

"The imperative tone of his voice stopped the fighting for a moment, but the leader, a great bully, roughly pushed back the officer and told him to go away or he would whip him. The officer again advanced and said, 'I arrest you,' attempting to place his hand on the man's shoulder, when the bully struck a fearful blow at the officer's face.

"This was parried, and instantly followed by a blow from the fist of the officer, striking the fellow under the chin and knocking him senseless. Blood issued from his mouth, nose and ears. It was believed that the man's neck was broken. A surgeon was called, who pronounced the case a critical one, and the wounded man was hurried away on a litter to the hospital.

"There the physicians said there was concussion of the brain, and that the man would die. All the medical skill that the officer could procure was employed in the hope of saving the life of the man. His conscience smote him for having, as he believed, taken the life of a fellow-creature, and he was inconsolable.

"Being on terms of intimacy with the President, about two o'clock that night the officer went to the White House, woke up Mr. Lincoln, and requested him to come into his office, where he told him his story. Mr. Lincoln listened with great interest until the narrative was completed, and then asked a few questions, after which he remarked:

"'I am sorry you had to kill the man, but these are times of war, and a great many men deserve killing. This one, according to your story, is one of them; so give yourself no uneasiness about the matter. I will stand by you.'

"'That is not why I came to you. I knew I did my duty, and had no fears of your disapproval of what I did,' replied the officer; and then he added: 'Why I came to you was, I felt great grief over the unfortunate affair, and I wanted to talk to you about it.'

"Mr. Lincoln then said, with a smile, placing his hand on the officer' shoulder: 'You go home now and get some sleep; but let me give you this piece of advice--hereafter, when you have occasion to strike a man, don't hit him with your fist; strike him with a club, a crowbar, or with something that won't kill him.'"

COULD BE ARBITRARY

Lincoln could be arbitrary when occasion required. This is the letter he wrote to one of the Department heads:

"You must make a job of it, and provide a place for the bearer of this, Elias Wampole. Make a job of it with the collector and have it done. You can do it for me, and you must."

There was no delay in taking action in this matter. Mr. Wampole, or "Eli," as he was thereafter known, "got there."

A GENERAL BUSTIFICATION

Many amusing stories are told of President Lincoln and his gloves. At about the time of his third reception he had on a tight-fitting pair of white kids, which he had with difficulty got on. He saw approaching in the distance an old Illinois friend named Simpson, whom he welcomed with a genuine Sangamon county (Illeenoy) shake, which resulted in bursting his white kid glove, with an audible sound. Then, raising his brawny hand up before him, looking at it with an indescribable expression, he said, while the whole procession was checked, witnessing this scene:

"Well, my old friend, this is a general bustification. You and I were never intended to wear these things. If they were stronger they might do well enough to keep out the cold, but they are a failure to shake hands with between old friends like us. Stand aside, Captain, and I'll see you shortly."

Simpson stood aside, and after the unwelcome ceremony was terminated he rejoined his old Illinois friend in familiar intercourse.

MAKING QUARTERMASTERS

H. C. Whitney wrote in 1866: "I was in Washington in the Indian service for a few days before August, 1861, and I merely said to President Lincoln one day: 'Everything is drifting into the war, and I guess you will have to put me in the army.'

"The President looked up from his work and said, good-humoredly:

'I'm making generals now; in a few days I will be making quartermasters, and then I'll fix you.'"

NO POSTMASTERS IN HIS POCKET

In the "Diary of a Public Man" appears this jocose anecdote:

"Mr. Lincoln walked into the corridor with us; and, as he bade us good-by and thanked Blank for what he had told him, he again brightened up for a moment and asked him in an abrupt kind of way, laying his hand as he spoke with a queer but not uncivil familiarity on his shoulder, 'You haven't such a thing as a postmaster in your pocket, have you?'

Blank stared at him in astonishment, and I thought a little in alarm, as if he suspected a sudden attack of insanity; then Mr. Lincoln went on:

'You see it seems to me kind of unnatural that you shouldn't have at least a postmaster in your pocket. Everybody I've seen for days past has had foreign ministers and collectors, and all kinds, and I thought you couldn't have got in here without having at least a postmaster get into your pocket!'"

HE "SKEWED" THE LINE

When a surveyor, Mr. Lincoln first platted the town of Petersburg, Ill. Some twenty or thirty years afterward the property-owners along one of the outlying streets had trouble in fixing their boundaries. They consulted the official plat and got no relief. A committee was sent to Springfield to consult the distinguished surveyor, but he failed to recall anything that would give them aid, and could only refer them to the record. The dispute therefore went into the courts. While the trial was pending, an old Irishman named McGuire, who had worked for some farmer during the summer, returned to town for the winter. The case being mentioned in his presence, he promptly said: "I can tell you all about it. I helped carry the chain when Abe Lincoln laid out this town. Over there where they are quarreling about the lines, when he was locating the street, he straightened up from his instrument and said: 'If I run that street right through, it will cut three or four feet off the end of --'s house. It's all he's got in the world and he never could get another. I reckon it won't hurt anything out here if I skew the line a little and miss him.'"

The line was "skewed," and hence the trouble, and more testimony furnished as to Lincoln's abounding kindness of heart, that would not willingly harm any human being.

"WHEREAS," HE STOLE NOTHING

One of the most celebrated courts-martial during the War was that of Franklin W. Smith and his brother, charged with defrauding the government. These men bore a high character for integrity. At this time, however, courts-martial were seldom invoked for any other purpose than to convict the accused, and the Smiths shared the usual fate of persons whose cases were submitted to such arbitrament. They were kept in prison, their papers seized, their business destroyed, and their reputations ruined, all of which was followed by a conviction.

The finding of the court was submitted to the President, who, after a careful investigation, disapproved the judgment, and wrote the following endorsement upon the papers:

"Whereas, Franklin W. Smith had transactions with the Navy Department to the amount of a millon and a quarter of dollars; and:

"Whereas, he had a chance to steal at least a quarter of a million and was only charged with stealing twenty-two hundred dollars, and the question now is about his stealing one hundred, I don't believe he stole anything at all.

"Therefore, the record and the findings are disapproved, declared null and void, and the defendants are fully discharged."

NOT LIKE THE POPE'S BULL

President Lincoln, after listening to the arguments and appeals of a committee which called upon him at the White House not long before the Emancipation Proclamation was issued, said:

"I do not want to issue a document that the whole world will see must necessarily be inoperative, like the Pope's bull against the comet."

COULD HE TELL?

A "high" private of the One Hundred and Fortieth Infantry Regiment, Pennsylvania Volunteers, wounded at Chancellorsville, was taken to Washington. One day, as he was becoming convalescent, a whisper ran down the long row of cots that the President was in the building and would soon pass by. Instantly every boy in blue who was able arose, stood erect, hands to the side, ready to salute his Commanderin-Chief.

The Pennsylvanian stood six feet seven inches in his stockings. Lincoln was six feet four. As the President approached this giant towering above him, he stopped in amazement, and casting his eyes from head to foot and from foot to head, as if contemplating the immense distance from one extremity to the other, he stood for a moment speechless.

At length, extending his hand, he exclaimed, "Hello, comrade, do you know when your feet get cold?"

"WHAT'S-HIS-NAME" GOT THERE.

General James B. Fry told a good one on Secretary of War Stanton, who was worsted in a contention with the President. Several brigadier-generals were to be selected, and Lincoln maintained that "something must be done in the interest of the Dutch." Many complaints had come from prominent men, born in the Fatherland, but who were fighting for the Union.

"Now, I want Schimmelpfennig given one of those brigadierships."

Stanton was stubborn and headstrong, as usual, but his manner and tone indicated that the President would have his own way in the end. However, he was not to be beaten without having made a fight.

"But, Mr. President," insisted the Iron War Secretary, "it may be that this Mr. Schim--what's-his-name--has no recommendations showing his fitness. Perhaps he can't speak English."

"That doesn't matter a bit, Stanton," retorted Lincoln, "he may be deaf and dumb for all I know, but whatever language he speaks, if any, we can furnish troops who will understand what he says. That name of his will make up for any differences in religion, politics or understanding, and I'll take the risk of his coming out all right."

Then, slamming his great hand upon the Secretary's desk, he said, "Schim-mel-fen-nig must be appointed."

And he was, there and then.

A REALLY GREAT GENERAL

"Do you know General A--?" queried the President one day to a friend who had "dropped in" at the White House.

"Certainly; but you are not wasting any time thinking about him, are you?" was the rejoinder.

"You wrong him," responded the President, "he is a really great man, a philosopher."

"How do you make that out? He isn't worth the powder and ball necessary to kill him so I have heard military men say," the friend remarked.

"He is a mighty thinker," the President returned, "because he has mastered that ancient and wise admonition, 'Know thyself;' he has formed an intimate acquaintance with himself, knows as well for what he is fitted and unfitted as any man living. Without doubt he is a remarkable man. This War has not produced another like him."

"How is it you are so highly pleased with General A-- all at once?"

"For the reason," replied Mr. Lincoln, with a merry twinkle of the eye, "greatly to my relief, and to the interests of the country, he has resigned. The country should express its gratitude in some substantial way."

"SHRUNK UP NORTH"

There was no member of the Cabinet from the South when Attorney-General Bates handed in his resignation, and President Lincoln had a great deal of trouble in making a selection. Finally Titian F. Coffey consented to fill the vacant place for a time, and did so until the appointment of Mr. Speed.

In conversation with Mr. Coffey the President quaintly remarked:

"My Cabinet has shrunk up North, and I must find a Southern man. I suppose if the twelve Apostles were to be chosen nowadays, the shrieks of locality would have to be heeded."

LINCOLN ADOPTED THE SUGGESTION

It is not generally known that President Lincoln adopted a suggestion made by Secretary of the Treasury Salmon P. Chase in regard to the Emancipation Proclamation, and incorporated it in that famous document.

After the President had read it to the members of the Cabinet he asked if he had omitted anything which should be added or inserted to strengthen it. It will be remembered that the closing paragraph of the Proclamation reads in this way:

"And upon this act, sincerely believed to be an act of justice warranted by the Constitution, I invoke the considerate judgment of mankind, and the gracious favor of Almighty God!" President Lincoln's draft of the paper ended with the word "mankind," and the words, "and the gracious favor of Almighty God," were those suggested by Secretary Chase.

SOMETHING FOR EVERYONE

It was the President's overweening desire to accommodate all persons who came to him soliciting favors, but the opportunity was never offered until an untimely and unthinking disease, which possessed many of the characteristics of one of the most dreaded maladies, confined him to his bed at the White House.

The rumor spread that the President was afflicted with this disease, while the truth was that it was merely a very mild attack of varioloid. The office-seekers didn't know the facts, and for once the Executive Mansion was clear of them.

One day, a man from the West, who didn't read the papers, but wanted the post office in his town, called at the White House. The President, being then practically a well man, saw him. The caller was engaged in a voluble endeavor to put his capabilities in the most favorable light, when the President interrupted him with the remark that he would be compelled to make the interview short, as his doctor was due.

"Why, Mr. President, are you sick?" queried the visitor.

"Oh, nothing much," replied Mr. Lincoln, "but the physician says he fears the worst."

"What worst, may I ask?"

"Smallpox," was the answer; "but you needn't be scared. I'm only in the first stages now."

The visitor grabbed his hat, sprang from his chair, and without a word bolted for the door.

"Don't be in a hurry," said the President placidly; "sit down and talk awhile."

"Thank you, sir; I'll call again," shouted the Westerner, as he disappeared through the opening in the wall.

"Now, that's the way with people," the President said, when relating the story afterward. "When I can't give them what they want, they're dissatisfied, and say harsh things about me; but when I've something to give to everybody they scamper off."

TOO MANY PIGS FOR THE TEATS

An applicant for a sutlership in the army relates this story: "In the winter of 1864, after serving three years in the Union Army, and being honorably discharged, I made application for the post sutlership at Point Lookout. My father being interested, we made application to Mr. Stanton, the Secretary of War. We obtained an audience, and were ushered into the presence of the most pompous man I ever met. As I entered he waved his hand for me to stop at a given distance from him, and then put these questions, viz.:

"'Did you serve three years in the army?'

"'I did, sir.'

"'Were you honorably discharged?'

"'I was, sir.'

"'Let me see your discharge.'

"I gave it to him. He looked it over, then said:

'Were you ever wounded?' I told him yes, at the battle of Williamsburg, May 5, 1861.

"He then said: 'I think we can give this position to a soldier who has lost an arm or leg, he being more deserving; and he then said I looked hearty and healthy enough to serve three years more. He would not give me a chance to argue my case.

The audience was at an end. He waved his hand to me. I was then dismissed from the august presence of the Honorable Secretary of War. "My father was waiting for me in the hallway, who saw by my countenance that I was not successful. I said to my father:

"'Let us go over to Mr. Lincoln; he may give us more satisfaction.'

"He said it would do me no good, but we went over. Mr. Lincoln's reception room was full of ladies and gentlemen when we entered.

"My turn soon came. Lincoln turned to my father and said

"'Now, gentlemen, be pleased to be as quick as possible with your business, as it is growing late.'

"My father then stepped up to Lincoln and introduced me to him. Lincoln then said:

"'Take a seat, gentlemen, and state your business as quickly as possible.'

"There was but one chair by Lincoln, so he motioned my father to sit, while I stood. My father stated the business to him as stated above. He then said:

"'Have you seen Mr. Stanton?'

"We told him yes, that he had refused. He (Mr. Lincoln) then said:

"'Gentlemen, this is Mr. Stanton's business; I cannot interfere with him; he attends to all these matters and I am sorry I cannot help you.'

"He saw that we were disappointed, and did his best to revive our spirits. He succeeded well with my father, who was a Lincoln man, and who was a staunch Republican.

"Mr. Lincoln then said:

"'Now, gentlemen, I will tell you, what it is; I have thousands of applications like this every day, but we cannot satisfy all for this reason, that these positions are like office seekers--there are too many pigs for the teats.'

"The ladies who were listening to the conversation placed their handkerchiefs to their faces and turned away. But the joke of 'Old Abe' put us all in a good humor. We then left the presence of the greatest and most just man who ever lived to fill the Presidential chair.'"

THE LAST TIME HE SAW DOUGLAS.

Speaking of his last meeting with Judge Douglas, Mr. Lincoln said: "One day Douglas came rushing in and said he had just got a telegraph dispatch from some friends in Illinois urging him to come out and help set things right in Egypt, and that he would go, or stay in Washington, just where I thought he could do the most good.

"I told him to do as he chose, but that probably he could do best in Illinois. Upon that he shook hands with me, and hurried away to catch the next train. I never saw him again."

HURT HIS LEGS LESS.

Lincoln was one of the attorneys in a case of considerable importance, court being held in a very small and dilapidated schoolhouse out in the country; Lincoln was compelled to stoop very much in order to enter the door, and the seats were so low that he doubled up his legs like a jackknife.

Lincoln was obliged to sit upon a school bench, and just in front of him was another, making the distance between him and the seat in front of him very narrow and uncomfortable.

His position was almost unbearable, and in order to carry out his preference which he secured as often as possible, and that was "to sit as near to the jury as convenient," he took advantage of his discomfort and finally said to the Judge on the "bench":

"Your Honor, with your permission, I'll sit up nearer to the gentlemen of the jury, for it hurts my legs less to rub my calves against the bench than it does to skin my shins."

A LITTLE SHY OR GRAMMAR

When Mr. Lincoln had prepared his brief letter accepting the Presidential nomination he took it to Dr. Newton Bateman, the State Superintendent of Education.

"Mr. Schoolmaster," he said, "here is my letter of acceptance. I am not very strong on grammar and I wish you to see if it is all right. I wouldn't like to have any mistakes in it.".

The doctor took the letter and after reading it, said:

"There is only one change I should suggest, Mr. Lincoln, you have written 'It shall be my care to not violate or disregard it in any part,' you should have written 'not to violate.' Never split an infinitive, is the rule."

Mr. Lincoln took the manuscript, regarding it a moment with a puzzled air, "So you think I better put those two little fellows end to end, do you?" he said as he made the change.

LIKELY TO DO IT

An officer, having had some trouble with General Sherman, being very angry, presented himself before Mr. Lincoln, who was visiting the camp, and said, "Mr. President, I have a cause of grievance. This morning I went to General Sherman and he threatened to shoot me."

"Threatened to shoot you?" asked Mr. Lincoln. "Well, (in a stage whisper) if I were you I would keep away from him; if he threatens to shoot, I would not trust him, for I believe he would do it."

"AND--HERE I AM!"

An old acquaintance of the President visited him in Washington. Lincoln desired to give him a place. Thus encouraged, the visitor, who was an honest man, but wholly inexperienced in public affairs or business, asked for a high office, Superintendent of the Mint.

The President was aghast, and said: "Good gracious! Why didn't he ask to be Secretary of the Treasury, and have done with it?"

Afterward, he said: "Well, now, I never thought Mr.-- had anything more than average ability, when we were young men together. But, then, I suppose he thought the same thing about me, and--here I am!"

SAFE AS LONG AS THEY WERE GOOD.

At the celebrated Peace Conference, whereat there was much "pow-wow" and no result, President Lincoln, in response to certain remarks by the Confederate commissioners, commented with some severity upon the conduct of the Confederate leaders, saying they had plainly forfeited all right to immunity from punishment for their treason.

Being positive and unequivocal in stating his views concerning individual treason, his words were of ominous import. There was a pause, during which Commissioner Hunter regarded the speaker with a steady, searching look. At length, carefully measuring his words, Mr. Hunter said:

"Then, Mr. President, if we understand you correctly, you think that we of the Confederacy have committed treason; are traitors to your Government; have forfeited our rights, and are proper subjects for the hangman. Is not that about what your words imply?"

"Yes," replied President Lincoln, "you have stated the proposition better than I did. That is about the size of it!"

Another pause, and a painful one succeeded, and then Hunter, with a pleasant smile remarked:

"Well, Mr. Lincoln, we have about concluded that we shall not be hanged as long as you are President--if we behave ourselves."

And Hunter meant what he said.

"SMELT NO ROYALTY IN OUR CARRIAGE"

On one occasion, in going to meet an appointment in the southern part of the Sucker State--that section of Illinois called Egypt--Lincoln, with other friends, was traveling in the "caboose" of a freight train, when the freight was switched off the main track to allow a special train to pass.

Lincoln's more aristocratic rival (Stephen A. Douglas) was being conveyed to the same town in this special. The passing train was decorated with banners and flags, and carried a band of music, which was playing "Hail to the Chief."

As the train whistled past, Lincoln broke out in a fit of laughter, and said: "Boys, the gentleman in that car evidently smelt no royalty in our carriage."

HELL A MILE FROM THE WHITE HOUSE

Ward Lamon told this story of President Lincoln, whom he found one day in a particularly gloomy frame of mind. Lamon said:

"The President remarked, as I came in, 'I fear I have made Senator Wade, of Ohio, my enemy for life.'

"'How?' I asked.

"'Well,' continued the President, 'Wade was here just now urging me to dismiss Grant, and, in response to something he said, I remarked, "Senator, that reminds me of a story."'

"'What did Wade say?' I inquired of the President.

"'He said, in a petulant way,' the President responded, '"It is with you, sir, all story, story! You are the father of every military blunder that has been made during the war. You are on your road to hell, sir, with this government, by your obstinacy, and you are not a mile off this minute."'

"'What did you say then?'

"'I good-naturedly said to him,' the President replied, '"Senator, that is just about from here to the Capitol, is it not?" He was very angry, grabbed up his hat and cane, and went away.'"

HIS "GLASS HACK"

President Lincoln had not been in the White House very long before Mrs. Lincoln became seized with the idea that a fine new barouche was about the proper thing for "the first lady in the land." The President did not care particularly about it one way or the other, and told his wife to order whatever she wanted.

Lincoln forgot all about the new vehicle, and was overcome with astonishment one afternoon when, having acceded to Mrs. Lincoln's desire to go driving, he found a beautiful barouche standing in front of the door of the White House.

His wife watched him with an amused smile, but the only remark he made was, "Well, Mary, that's about the slickest 'glass hack' in town, isn't it?"

LEAVE HIM KICKING

Lincoln, in the days of his youth, was often unfaithful to his Quaker traditions. On the day of election in 1840, word came to him that one Radford, a Democratic contractor, had taken possession of one of the polling places with his workmen, and was preventing the Whigs from voting. Lincoln started off at a gait which showed his interest in the matter in hand.

He went up to Radford and persuaded him to leave the polls, remarking at the same time: "Radford, you'll spoil and blow, if you live much longer."

Radford's prudence prevented an actual collision, which, it is said, Lincoln regretted. He told his friend Speed he wanted Radford to show fight so that he might "knock him down and leave him kicking."

"WHO COMMENCED THIS FUSS?"

President Lincoln was at all times an advocate of peace, provided it could be obtained honorably and with credit to the United States. As to the cause of the Civil War, which side of Mason and Dixon's line was responsible for it, who fired the first shots, who were the aggressors, etc., Lincoln did not seem to bother about; he wanted to preserve the Union, above all things. Slavery, he was assured, was dead, but he thought the former slaveholders should be recompensed.

To illustrate his feelings in the matter he told this story:

"Some of the supporters of the Union cause are opposed to accommodate or yield to the South in any manner or way because the Confederates began the war; were determined to take their States out of the Union, and, consequently, should be held responsible to the last stage for whatever may come in the future. Now this reminds me of a good story I heard once, when I lived in Illinois.

"A vicious bull in a pasture took after everybody who tried to cross the lot, and one day a neighbor of the owner was the victim. This man was a speedy fellow and got to a friendly tree ahead of the bull, but not in time to climb the tree. So he led the enraged animal a merry race around the tree, finally succeeding in seizing the bull by the tail.

"The bull, being at a disadvantage, not able to either catch the man or release his tail, was mad enough to eat nails; he dug up the earth with his feet, scattered gravel all around, bellowed until you could hear him for two miles or more, and at length broke into a dead run, the man hanging onto his tail all the time.

"While the bull, much out of temper, was legging it to the best of his ability, his tormentor, still clinging to the tail, asked, 'Darn you, who commenced this fuss?'

"It's our duty to settle this fuss at the earliest possible moment, no matter who commenced it. That's my idea of it."

"ABE'S" LITTLE JOKE

When General W. T. Sherman, November 12th, 1864, severed all communication with the North and started for Savannah with his magnificent army of sixty thousand men, there was much anxiety for a month as to his whereabouts. President Lincoln, in response to an inquiry, said: "I know what hole Sherman went in at, but I don't know what hole he'll come out at."

Colonel McClure had been in consultation with the President one day, about two weeks after Sherman's disappearance, and in this connection related this incident

"I was leaving the room, and just as I reached the door the President turned around, and, with a merry twinkling of the eye, inquired, 'McClure, wouldn't you like to hear something from Sherman?'

"The inquiry electrified me at the instant, as it seemed to imply that Lincoln had some information on the subject. I immediately answered, 'Yes, most of all, I should like to hear from Sherman.'

"To this President Lincoln answered, with a hearty laugh: 'Well, I'll be hanged if I wouldn't myself.'"

WHAT SUMMER THOUGHT

Although himself a most polished, even a fastidious, gentleman, Senator Sumner never allowed Lincoln's homely ways to hide his great qualities. He gave him a respect and esteem at the start which others accorded only after experience. The Senator was most tactful, too, in his dealings with Mrs. Lincoln, and soon had a firm footing in the household. That he was proud of this, perhaps a little boastful, there is no doubt.

Lincoln himself appreciated this. "Sumner thinks he runs me," he said, with an amused twinkle, one day.

A USELESS DOG

When Hood's army had been scattered into fragments, President Lincoln, elated by the defeat of what had so long been a menacing force on the borders of Tennessee was reminded by its collapse of the fate of a savage dog belonging to one of his neighbors in the frontier settlements in which he lived in his youth. "The dog," he said, "was the terror of the neighborhood, and its owner, a churlish and quarrelsome fellow, took pleasure in the brute's forcible attitude.

"Finally, all other means having failed to subdue the creature, a man loaded a lump of meat with a charge of powder, to which was attached a slow fuse; this was dropped where the dreaded dog would find it, and the animal gulped down the tempting bait.

"There was a dull rumbling, a muffled explosion, and fragments of the dog were seen flying in every direction. The grieved owner, picking up the shattered remains of his cruel favorite, said: 'He was a good dog, but as a dog, his days of usefulness are over.' Hood's army was a good army," said Lincoln, by way of comment, "and we were all afraid of it, but as an army, its usefulness is gone."

ORIGIN OF THE "INFLUENCE" STORY

Judge Baldwin, of California, being in Washington, called one day on General Halleck, then Commander-in-Chief of the Union forces, and, presuming upon a familiar acquaintance in California a few years since, solicited a pass outside of our lines to see a brother in Virginia, not thinking that he would meet with a refusal, as both his brother and himself were good Union men.

"We have been deceived too often," said General Halleck, "and I regret I can't grant it."

Judge B. then went to Stanton, and was very briefly disposed of with the same result. Finally, he obtained an interview with Mr. Lincoln, and stated his case.

"Have you applied to General Halleck?" inquired the President.

"Yes, and met with a flat refusal," said Judge B.

"Then you must see Stanton," continued the President.

"I have, and with the same result," was the reply.

"Well, then," said Mr. Lincoln, with a smile, "I can do nothing; for you must know that I have very little influence with this Administration, although I hope to have more with the next."

FELT SORRY FOR BOTH

Many ladies attended the famous debates between Lincoln and Douglas, and they were the most unprejudiced listeners. "I can recall only one fact of the debates," says Mrs. William Crotty, of Seneca, Illinois, "that I felt so sorry for Lincoln while Douglas was speaking, and then to my surprise I felt so sorry for Douglas when Lincoln replied."

The disinterested to whom it was an intellectual game, felt the power and charm of both men.

WHERE DID IT COME FROM?

"What made the deepest impression upon you?" inquired a friend one day, "when you stood in the presence of the Falls of Niagara, the greatest of natural wonders?"

"The thing that struck me most forcibly when I saw the Falls," Lincoln responded, with characteristic deliberation, "was, where in the world did all that water come from?"

"ALL SICKER'N YOUR MAN"

A Commissioner to the Hawaiian Islands was to be appointed, and eight applicants had filed their papers, when a delegation from the South appeared at the White House on behalf of a ninth. Not only was their man fit--so the delegation urged--but was also in bad health, and a residence in that balmy climate would be of great benefit to him.

The President was rather impatient that day, and before the members of the delegation had fairly started in, suddenly closed the interview with this remark:

"Gentlemen, I am sorry to say that there are eight other applicants for that place, and they are all 'sicker'n' your man."

EASIER TO EMPTY THE POTOMAC

An officer of low volunteer rank persisted in telling and re-telling his troubles to the President on a summer afternoon when Lincoln was tired and careworn.

After listening patiently, he finally turned upon the man, and, looking wearily out upon the broad Potomac in the distance, said in a peremptory tone that ended the interview:

"Now, my man, go away, go away. I cannot meddle in your case. I could as easily bail out the Potomac River with a teaspoon as attend to all the details of the army."

HE WANTED A STEADY HAND

When the Emancipation Proclamation was taken to Mr. Lincoln by Secretary Seward, for the President's signature, Mr. Lincoln took a pen, dipped it in the ink, moved his hand to the place for the signature, held it a moment, then removed his hand and dropped the pen. After a little hesitation, he again took up the pen and went through the same movement as before. Mr. Lincoln then turned to Mr. Seward and said:

"I have been shaking hands since nine o'clock this morning, and my right arm is almost paralyzed. If my name ever goes into history, it will be for this act, and my whole soul is in it. If my hand trembles when I sign the Proclamation, all who examine the document hereafter will say, 'He hesitated.'"

He then turned to the table, took up the pen again, and slowly, firmly wrote "Abraham Lincoln," with which the whole world is now familiar.

He then looked up, smiled, and said, "That will do."

LINCOLN SAW STANTON ABOUT IT

Mr. Lovejoy, heading a committee of Western men, discussed an important scheme with the President, and the gentlemen were then directed to explain it to Secretary of War Stanton.

Upon presenting themselves to the Secretary, and showing the President's order, the Secretary said: "Did Lincoln give you an order of that kind?"

"He did, sir."

"Then he is a d--d fool," said the angry Secretary.

"Do you mean to say that the President is a d--d fool?" asked Lovejoy, in amazement.

"Yes, sir, if he gave you such an order as that."

The bewildered Illinoisan betook himself at once to the President and related the result of the conference.

"Did Stanton say I was a d--d fool?" asked Lincoln at the close of the recital.

"He did, sir, and repeated it."

After a moment's pause, and looking up, the President said: "If Stanton said I was a d--d fool, then I must be one, for he is nearly always right, and generally says what he means. I will slip over and see him."

MRS. LINCOLN'S SURPRISE

A good story is told of how Mrs. Lincoln made a little surprise for her husband.

In the early days it was customary for lawyers to go from one county to another on horseback, a journey which often required several weeks. On returning from one of these trips, late one night, Mr. Lincoln dismounted from his horse at the familiar corner and then turned to go into the house, but stopped; a perfectly unknown structure was before him. Surprised, and thinking there must be some mistake, he went across the way and knocked at a neighbor's door. The family had retired, and so called out:

"Who's there?"

"Abe Lincoln," was the reply. "I am looking for my house. I thought it was across the way, but when I went away a few weeks ago there was only a one-story house there and now there is a two-story house in its place. I think I must be lost."

The neighbors then explained that Mrs. Lincoln had added another story during his absence. And Mr. Lincoln laughed and went to his remodeled house.

MENACE TO THE GOVERNMENT

The persistence of office-seekers nearly drove President Lincoln wild. They slipped in through the half-opened doors of the Executive Mansion; they dogged his steps if he walked; they edged their way through the crowds and thrust their papers in his hands when he rode; and, taking it all in all, they well-nigh worried him to death.

He once said that if the Government passed through the Rebellion without dismemberment there was the strongest danger of its falling a prey to the rapacity of the office-seeking class.

"This human struggle and scramble for office, for a way to live without work, will finally test the strength of our institutions," were the words he used.

TROOPS COULDN'T FLY OVER IT

On April 20th a delegation from Baltimore appeared at the White House and begged the President that troops for Washington be sent around and not through Baltimore.

President Lincoln replied, laughingly: "If I grant this concession, you will be back tomorrow asking that no troops be marched 'around' it."

The President was right. That afternoon, and again on Sunday and Monday, committees sought him, protesting that Maryland soil should not be "polluted" by the feet of soldiers marching against the South.

The President had but one reply: "We must have troops, and as they can neither crawl under Maryland nor fly over it, they must come across it."

PAT WAS "FORNINST THE GOVERNMENT"

The Governor-General of Canada, with some of his principal officers, visited President Lincoln in the summer of 1864.

They had been very troublesome in harboring blockade runners, and they were said to have carried on a large trade from their ports with the Confederates. Lincoln treated his guests with great courtesy.

After a pleasant interview, the Governor, alluding to the coming Presidential election said, jokingly, but with a grain of sarcasm: "I understand Mr. President, that everybody votes in this country. If we remain until November, can we vote?"

"You remind me, replied the President, "of a countryman of yours, a green emigrant from Ireland. Pat arrived on election day, and perhaps was as eager a your Excellency to vote, and to vote early, and late and often.

"So, upon landing at Castle Garden, he hastened to the nearest voting place, and as he approached, the judge who received the ballots inquired, 'Who do you want to vote for? On which side are you?' Poor Pat was embarrassed; he did not know who were the candidates. He stopped, scratched his head, then, with the readiness of his countrymen, he said:

"'I am forninst the Government, anyhow. Tell me, if your Honor plase: which is the rebellion side, and I'll tell you haw I want to vote. In ould Ireland, I was always on the rebellion side, and, by Saint Patrick, I'll do that same in America.' Your Excellency," said Mr. Lincoln, "would, I should think, not be at all at a loss on which side to vote!"

"CAN'T SPARE THIS MAN"

One night, about eleven o'clock, Colonel A. K. McClure, whose intimacy with President Lincoln was so great that he could obtain admittance to the Executive Mansion at any and all hours, called at the White House to urge Mr. Lincoln to remove General Grant from command.

After listening patiently for a long time, the President, gathering himself up in his chair, said, with the utmost earnestness:

"I can't spare this man; he fights!"

In relating the particulars of this interview, Colonel McClure said:

"That was all he said, but I knew that it was enough, and that Grant was safe in Lincoln's hands against his countless hosts of enemies. The only man in all the nation who had the power to save Grant was Lincoln, and he had decided to do it. He was not influenced by any personal partiality for Grant, for they had never met.

"It was not until after the battle of Shiloh, fought on the 6th and 7th of April, 1862, that Lincoln was placed in a position to exercise a controlling influence in shaping the destiny of Grant. The first reports from the Shiloh battle-field created profound alarm throughout the entire country, and the wildest exaggerations were spread in a floodtide of vituperation against Grant.

"The few of to-day who can recall the inflamed condition of public sentiment against Grant caused by the disastrous first day's battle at Shiloh will remember that he was denounced as incompetent for his command by the public journals of all parties in the North, and with almost entire unanimity by Senators and Congressmen, regardless of political affinities.

"I appealed to Lincoln for his own sake to remove Grant at once, and in giving my reasons for it I simply voiced the admittedly overwhelming protest from the loyal people of the land against Grant's continuance in command.

"I did not forget that Lincoln was the one man who never allowed himself to appear as wantonly defying public sentiment. It seemed to me impossible for him to save Grant without taking a crushing load of condemnation upon himself; but Lincoln was wiser than all those around him, and he not only saved Grant, but he saved him by such well-concerted effort that he soon won popular applause from those who were most violent in demanding Grant's dismissal."

HIS TEETH CHATTERED

During the Lincoln-Douglas joint debates of 1858, the latter accused Lincoln of having, when in Congress, voted against the appropriation for supplies to be sent the United States soldiers in Mexico. In reply, Lincoln said: "This is a perversion of the facts. I was opposed to the policy of the administration in declaring war against Mexico; but when war was declared I never failed to vote for the support of any proposition looking to the comfort of our poor fellows who were maintaining the dignity of our flag in a war that I thought unnecessary and unjust."

He gradually became more and more excited; his voice thrilled and his whole frame shook. Sitting on the stand was O. B. Ficklin, who had served in Congress with Lincoln in 1847. Lincoln reached back, took Ficklin by the coat-collar, back of his neck, and in no gentle manner lifted him from his seat as if he had been a kitten, and roared: "Fellow-citizens, here is Ficklin, who was at that time in Congress with me, and he knows it is a lie."

He shook Ficklin until his teeth chattered. Fearing he would shake Ficklin's head off, Ward Lamon grasped Lincoln's hand and broke his grip.

After the speaking was over, Ficklin, who had warm personal friendship with him, said: "Lincoln, you nearly shook all the Democracy out of me to-day."

"AARON GOT HIS COMMISSION"

President Lincoln was censured for appointing one that had zealously opposed his second term.

He replied: "Well, I suppose Judge E., having been disappointed before, did behave pretty ugly, but that wouldn't make him any less fit for the place; and I think I have Scriptural authority for appointing him.

"You remember when the Lord was on Mount Sinai getting out a commission for Aaron, that same Aaron was at the foot of the mountain making a false god for the people to worship. Yet Aaron got his commission, you know."

LINCOLN AND THE MINISTERS

At the time of Lincoln's nomination, at Chicago, Mr. Newton Bateman, Superintendent of Public Instruction for the State of Illinois, occupied a room adjoining and opening into the Executive Chamber at Springfield. Frequently this door was open during Mr. Lincoln's receptions, and throughout the seven months or more of his occupation he saw him nearly every day. Often, when Mr. Lincoln was tired, he closed the door against all intruders, and called Mr. Bateman into his room for a quiet talk. On one of these occasions, Mr. Lincoln took up a book containing canvass of the city of Springfield, in which he lived, showing the candidate for whom each citizen had declared it his intention to vote in the approaching election. Mr.Lincoln's friends had, doubtless at his own request, placed the result of the canvass in his hands. This was towards the close of October, and only a few days before election. Calling Mr. Bateman to a seat by his side, having previously locked all the doors, he said:

"Let us look over this book; I wish particularly to see how the ministers if Springfield are going to vote." The leaves were turned, one by one, and as the names were examined Mr. Lincoln frequently asked if this one and that one was not a minister, or an elder, or a member of such and such a church, and sadly expressed his surprise on receiving an affirmative answer. In that manner he went through the book, and then he closed it, and sat silently for some minutes regarding a memorandum in pencil which lay before him. At length he turned to Mr. Bateman, with a face full of sadness, and said:

"Here are twenty-three ministers of different denominations, and all of them are against me but three, and here are a great many prominent members of churches, a very large majority are against me. Mr. Bateman, I am not a Christian--God knows I would be one --but I have carefully read the Bible, and I do not so understand this book," and he drew forth a pocket New Testament.

"These men well know," he continued, "that I am for freedom in the Territories, freedom everywhere, as free as the Constitution and the laws will permit, and that my opponents are for slavery. They know this, and yet, with this book in their hands, in the light of which human bondage cannot live a moment, they are going to vote against me; I do not understand it at all."

Here Mr. Lincoln paused--paused for long minutes, his features surcharged with emotion. Then he rose and walked up and down the reception-room in the effort to retain or regain his self-possession. Stopping at last, he said, with a trembling voice and cheeks wet with tears:

"I know there is a God, and that He hates injustice and slavery. I see the storm coming, and I know that His hand is in it. If He has a place and work for me, and I think He has, I believe I am ready. I am nothing, but Truth is everything. I know I am right, because I know that liberty is right, for Christ teaches it, and Christ is God. I have told them that a house divided against itself cannot stand; and Christ and Reason say the same, and they will find it so.

"Douglas doesn't care whether slavery is voted up or down, but God cares, and humanity cares, and I care; and with God's help I shall not fail. I may not see the end, but it will come, and I shall be vindicated; and these men will find they have not read their Bible right."

Much of this was uttered as if he were speaking to himself, and with a sad, earnest solemnity of manner impossible to be described. After a pause he resumed:

"Doesn't it seem strange that men can ignore the moral aspect of this contest? No revelation could make it plainer to me that slavery or the Government must be destroyed. The future would be something awful, as I look at it, but for this rock on which I stand" (alluding to the Testament which he still held in his hand), "especially with the knowledge of how these ministers are going to vote. It seems as if God had borne with this thing (slavery) until the teachers of religion have come to defend it from the Bible, and to claim for it a divine character and sanction; and now the cup of iniquity is full, and the vials of wrath will be poured out."

Everything he said was of a peculiarly deep, tender, and religious tone, and all was tinged with a touching melancholy. He repeatedly referred to his conviction that the day of wrath was at hand, and that he was to be an actor in the terrible struggle which would issue in the overthrow of slavery, although he might not live to see the end.

After further reference to a belief in the Divine Providence and the fact of God in history, the conversation turned upon prayer. He freely stated his belief in the duty, privilege, and efficacy of prayer, and intimated, in no unmistakable terms, that he had sought in that way Divine guidance and favor. The effect of this conversation upon the mind of Mr. Bateman, a Christian gentleman whom Mr. Lincoln profoundly respected, was to convince him that Mr. Lincoln had, in a quiet way, found a path to the Christian standpoint--that he had found God, and rested on the eternal truth of God. As the two men were about to separate, Mr. Bateman remarked:

"I have not supposed that you were accustomed to think so much upon this class of subjects; certainly your friends generally are ignorant of the sentiments you have expressed to me."

He replied quickly: "I know they are, but I think more on these subjects than upon all others, and I have done so for years; and I am willing you should know it."

HARDTACK BETTER THAN GENERALS

Secretary of War Stanton told the President the following story, which greatly amused the latter, as he was especially fond of a joke at the expense of some high military or civil dignitary.

Stanton had little or no sense of humor.

When Secretary Stanton was making a trip up the Broad River in North Carolina, in a tugboat, a Federal picket yelled out, "What have you got on board of that tug?"

The severe and dignified answer was, "The Secretaty of War and Major-General Foster."

Instantly the picket roared back, "We've got Major-Generals enough up here. Why don't you bring us up some hardtack?"

GOT THE PREACHER

A story told by a Cabinet member tended to show how accurately Lincoln could calculate political results in advance--a faculty which remained with him all his life.

"A friend, who was a Democrat, had come to him early in the canvass and told him he wanted to see him elected, but did not like to vote against his party; still he would vote for him, if the contest was to be so close that every vote was needed.

"A short time before the election Lincoln said to him: 'I have got the preacher, and I don't want your vote.'"

BIG JOKE ON HALLECK

When General Halleck was Commander-in-Chief of the Union forces, with headquarters at Washington, President Lincoln unconsciously played a big practical joke upon that dignified officer. The President had spent the night at the Soldiers' Home, and the next morning asked Captain Derickson, commanding the company of Pennsylvania soldiers, which was the Presidential guard at the White House and the Home--wherever the President happened to be --to go to town with him.

Captain Derickson told the story in a most entertaining way:
"When we entered the city, Mr. Lincoln said he would call at General Halleck's headquarters and get what news had been received from the army during the night. I informed him that General Cullum, chief aid to General Halleck, was raised in Meadville, and that I knew him when I was a boy.

"He replied, 'Then we must see both the gentlemen.' When the carriage stopped, he requested me to remain seated, and said he would bring the gentlemen down to see me, the office being on the second floor. In a short time the President came down, followed by the other gentlemen. When he introduced them to me, General Cullum recognized and seemed pleased to see me.

"In General Halleck I thought I discovered a kind of quizzical look, as much as to say, 'Isn't this rather a big joke to ask the Commander-in-Chief of the army down to the street to be introduced to a country captain?'"

STORIES BETTER THAN DOCTORS

A gentleman, visiting a hospital at Washington, heard an occupant of one of the beds laughing and talking about the President, who had been there a short time before and gladdened the wounded with some of his stories. The soldier seemed in such good spirits that the gentleman inquired:

"You must be very slightly wounded?"

"Yes," replied the brave fellow, "very slightly--I have only lost one leg, and I'd be glad enough to lose the other, if I could hear some more of 'Old Abe's' stories."

MR. BULL DIDN'T GET HIS COTTON.

Because of the blockade, by the Union fleets, of the Southern cotton ports, England was deprived of her supply of cotton, and scores of thousands of British operatives were thrown out of employment by the closing of the cotton mills at Manchester and other cities in Great Britain. England (John Bull) felt so badly about this that the British wanted to go to war on account of it, but when the United States eagle ruffled up its wings the English thought over the business and concluded not to fight.

"Harper's Weekly" of May 16th, 1863, contained the cartoon we reproduce, which shows John Bull as manifesting much anxiety regarding the cotton he had bought from the Southern planters, but which the latter could not deliver. Beneath the cartoon is this bit of dialogue between John Bull and President Lincoln: MR. BULL (confiding creature): "Hi want my cotton, bought at fi'pence a pound."

MR. LINCOLN: "Don't know anything about it, my dear sir. Your friends, the rebels, are burning all the cotton they can find, and I confiscate the rest. Good-morning, John!"

As President Lincoln has a big fifteen-inch gun at his side, the black muzzle of which is pressed tightly against Mr. Bull's waistcoat, the President, to all appearances, has the best of the argument "by a long shot." Anyhow, Mr. Bull had nothing more to say, but gave the cotton matter up as a bad piece of business, and pocketed the loss.

STICK TO AMERICAN PRINCIPLES.

President Lincoln's first conclusion (that Mason and Slidell should be released) was the real ground on which the Administration submitted. "We must stick to American principles concerning the rights of neutrals." It was to many, as Secretary of the Treasury Chase declared it was to him, "gall and wormwood." James Russell Lowell's verse expressed best the popular feeling:

We give the critters back, John, Cos Abram thought 'twas right; It warn't your bullyin' clack, John, Provokin' us to fight.

The decision raised Mr. Lincoln immeasurably in the view of thoughtful men, especially in England.

USED "RUDE TACT"

General John C. Fremont, with headquarters at St. Louis, astonished the country by issuing a proclamation declaring, among other things, that the property, real and personal, of all the persons in the State of Missouri who should take up arms against the United States, or who should be directly proved to have taken an active part with its enemies in the field, would be confiscated to public use and their slaves, if they had any, declared freemen.

The President was dismayed; he modified that part of the proclamation referring to slaves, and finally replaced Fremont with General Hunter.

Mrs. Fremont (daughter of Senator T. H. Benton), her husband's real chief of staff, flew to Washington and sought Mr. Lincoln. It was midnight, but the President gave her an audience. Without waiting for an explanation, she violently charged him with sending an enemy to Missouri to look into Fremont's case, and threatening that if Fremont desired to he could set up a government for himself.

"I had to exercise all the rude tact I have to avoid quarreling with her," said Mr. Lincoln afterwards.

"ABE" ON A WOODPILE.

Lincoln's attempt to make a lawyer of himself under adverse and unpromising circumstances--he was a bare-footed farm-hand --excited comment. And it was not to be wondered. One old man, who was yet alive as late as 1901, had often employed Lincoln to do farm work for him, and was surprised to find him one day sitting barefoot on the summit of a woodpile and attentively reading a book.

"This being an unusual thing for farm-hands in that early day to do," said the old man, when relating the story, "I asked him what he was reading.

"'I'm not reading,' he answered. 'I'm studying.'

"'Studying what?' I inquired.

"'Law, sir,' was the emphatic response.

"It was really too much for me, as I looked at him sitting there proud as Cicero. 'Great God Almighty!' I exclaimed, and passed on." Lincoln merely laughed and resumed his "studies."

TAKING DOWN A DANDY

In a political campaign, Lincoln once replied to Colonel Richard Taylor, a self-conceited, dandified man, who wore a gold chain and ruffled shirt. His party at that time was posing as the hard-working bone and sinew of the land, while the Whigs were stigmatized as aristocrats, ruffled-shirt gentry. Taylor making a sweeping gesture, his overcoat became torn open, displaying his finery. Lincoln in reply said, laying his hand on his jeans-clad breast:

"Here is your aristocrat, one of your silk-stocking gentry, at your service." Then, spreading out his hands, bronzed and gaunt with toil:

"Here is your rag-basin with lily-white hands. Yes, I suppose, according to my friend Taylor, I am a bloated aristocrat."

WANTED TO "BORROW" THE ARMY

During one of the periods when things were at a standstill, the Washington authorities, being unable to force General McClellan to assume an aggressive attitude, President Lincoln went to the general's headquarters to have a talk with him, but for some reason he was unable to get an audience.

Mr. Lincoln returned to the White House much disturbed at his failure to see the commander of the Union forces, and immediately sent for two general officers, to have a consultation. On their arrival, he told them he must have some one to talk to about the situation, and as he had failed to see General McClellan, he wished their views as to the possibility or probability of commencing active operations with the Army of the Potomac.

"Something's got to be done," said the President, emphatically, "and done right away, or the bottom will fall out of the whole thing. Now, if McClellan doesn't want to use the army for awhile, I'd like to borrow it from him and see if I can't do something or other with it.

"If McClellan can't fish, he ought at least to be cutting bait at a time like this."

YOUNG "SUCKER" VISITORS

After Mr. Lincoln's nomination for the Presidency, the Executive Chamber, a large, fine room in the State House at Springfield, was set apart for him, where he met the public until after his election.

As illustrative of the nature of many of his calls, the following incident was related by Mr. Holland, an eye-witness: "Mr. Lincoln being in conversation with a gentleman one day, two raw, plainly-dressed young 'Suckers' entered the room, and bashfully lingered near the door. As soon as he observed them, and saw their embarrassment, he rose and walked to them, saying: 'How do you do, my good fellows? What can I do for you? Will you sit down?' The spokesman of the pair, the shorter of the two, declined to sit, and explained the object of the call thus: He had had a talk about the relative height of Mr. Lincoln and his companion, and had asserted his belief that they were of exactly the same height. He had come in to verify his judgment. Mr. Lincoln smiled, went and got his cane, and, placing the end of it upon the wall, said" 'Here, young man, come under here.' "The young man came under the cane as Mr. Lincoln held it, and when it was perfectly adjusted to his height, Mr. Lincoln said:

"'Now, come out, and hold the cane.'

"This he did, while Mr. Lincoln stood under. Rubbing his head back and forth to see that it worked easily under the measurement, he stepped out, and declared to the sagacious fellow who was curiously looking on, that he had guessed with remarkable accuracy--that he and the young man were exactly the same height. Then he shook hands with them and sent them on their way. Mr. Lincoln would just as soon have thought of cutting off his right hand as he would have thought of turning those boys away with the impression that they had in any way insulted his dignity.

"AND YOU DON'T WEAR HOOPSKIRTS"

An Ohio Senator had an appointment with President Lincoln at six o'clock, and as he entered the vestibule of the White House his attention was attracted toward a poorly clad young woman, who was violently sobbing. He asked her the cause of her distress. She said she had been ordered away by the servants, after vainly waiting many hours to see the President about her only brother, who had been condemned to death. Her story was this:

She and her brother were foreigners, and orphans. They had been in this country several years. Her brother enlisted in the army, but, through bad influences, was induced to desert. He was captured, tried and sentenced to be shot--the old story.

The poor girl had obtained the signatures of some persons who had formerly known him, to a petition for a pardon, and alone had come to Washington to lay the case before the President. Thronged as the waiting-rooms always were, she had passed the long hours of two days trying in vain to get an audience, and had at length been ordered away.

The gentleman's feelings were touched. He said to her that he had come to see the President, but did not know as he should succeed. He told her, however, to follow him upstairs, and he would see what could be done for her.

Just before reaching the door, Mr. Lincoln came out, and, meeting his friend, said good-humoredly, "Are you not ahead of time?" The gentleman showed him his watch, with the hand upon the hour of six.

"Well," returned Mr. Lincoln, "I have been so busy to-day that I have not had time to get a lunch. Go in and sit down; I will be back directly."

The gentleman made the young woman accompany him into the office, and when they were seated, said to her: "Now, my good girl, I want you to muster all the courage you have in the world. When the President comes back, he will sit down in that armchair. I shall get up to speak to him, and as I do so you must force yourself between us, and insist upon his examination of your papers, telling him it is a case of life and death, and admits of no delay." These instructions were carried out to the letter. Mr. Lincoln was at first somewhat surprised at the apparent forwardness of the young woman, but observing her distressed appearance, he ceased conversation with his friend, and commenced an examination of the document she had placed in his hands.

Glancing from it to the face of the petitioner, whose tears had broken forth afresh, he studied its expression for a moment, and then his eye fell upon her scanty but neat dress. Instantly his face lighted up.

"My poor girl," said he, "you have come here with no Governor, or Senator, or member of Congress to plead your cause. You seem honest and truthful; and you don't wear hoopskirts--and I will be whipped but I will pardon your brother." And he did.

LIEUTENANT TAD LINCOLN'S SENTINELS

President Lincoln's favorite son, Tad, having been sportively commissioned a lieutenant in the United States Army by Secretary Stanton, procured several muskets and drilled the men-servants of the house in the manual of arms without attracting the attention of his father. And one night, to his consternation, he put them all on duty, and relieved the regular sentries, who, seeing the lad in full uniform, or perhaps appreciating the joke, gladly went to their quarters. His brother objected; but Tad insisted upon his rights as an officer. The President laughed but declined to interfere, but when the lad had lost his little authority in his boyish sleep, the Commander-in-Chief of the Army and Navy of the United States went down and personally discharged the sentries his son had put on the post.

DOUGLAS HELD LINCOLN'S HAT

When Mr. Lincoln delivered his first inaugural he was introduced by his friend, United States Senator E. D. Baker, of Oregon. He carried a cane and a little roll--the manuscript of his inaugural address. There was moment's pause after the introduction, as he vainly looked for a spot where he might place his high silk hat.

Stephen A. Douglas, the political antagonist of his whole public life, the man who had pressed him hardest in the campaign of 1860, was seated just behind him. Douglas stepped forward quickly, and took the hat which Mr. Lincoln held helplessly in his hand.

"If I can't be President," Douglas whispered smilingly to Mrs. Brown, a cousin of Mrs. Lincoln and a member of the President's party, "I at least can hold his hat."

THE DEAD MAN SPOKE.

Mr. Lincoln once said in a speech: "Fellow-citizens, my friend, Mr. Douglas, made the startling announcement to-day that the Whigs are all dead.

"If that be so, fellow-citizens, you will now experience the novelty of hearing a speech from a dead man; and I suppose you might properly say, in the language of the old hymn

"'Hark! from the tombs a doleful sound.'"

MILITARY SNAILS NOT SPEEDY

President Lincoln--as he himself put it in conversation one day with a friend--"fairly ached" for his generals to "get down to business." These slow generals he termed "snails."

Grant, Sherman and Sheridan were his favorites, for they were aggressive. They did not wait for the enemy to attack. Too many of the others were "lingerers," as Lincoln called them. They were magnificent in defense, and stubborn and brave, but their names figured too much on the "waiting list."

The greatest fault Lincoln found with so many of the commanders on the Union side was their unwillingness to move until everything was exactly to their liking.

Lincoln could not understand why these leaders of Northern armies hesitated.

OUTRAN THE JACK-RABBIT

When the Union forces were routed in the first battle of Bull Run, there were many civilians present, who had gone out from Washington to witness the battle. Among the number were several Congressmen. One of these was a tall, long-legged fellow, who wore a long-tailed coat and a high plug hat. When the retreat began, this Congressman was in the lead of the entire crowd fleeing toward Washington. He outran all the rest, and was the first man to arrive in the city. No person ever made such good use of long legs as this Congressman. His immense stride carried him yards at every bound. He went over ditches and gullies at a single leap, and cleared a six-foot fence with a foot to spare. As he went over the fence his plug hat blew off, but he did not pause. With his long coat-tails flying in the wind, he continued straight ahead for Washington.

Many of those behind him were scared almost to death, but the flying Congressman was such a comical figure that they had to laugh in spite of their terror.

Mr. Lincoln enjoyed the description of how this Congressman led the race from Bull's Run, and laughed at it heartily.

"I never knew but one fellow who could run like that," he said, "and he was a young man out in Illinois. He had been sparking a girl, much against the wishes of her father. In fact, the old man took such a dislike to him that he threatened to shoot him if he ever ought him around his premises again.

"One evening the young man learned that the girl's father had gone to the city, and he ventured out to the house. He was sitting in the parlor, with his arm around Betsy's waist, when he suddenly spied the old man coming around the corner of the house with a shotgun. Leaping through a window into the garden, he started down a path at the top of his speed. He was a long-legged fellow, and could run like greased lightning. Just then a jack-rabbit jumped up in the path in front of him. In about two leaps he overtook the rabbit. Giving it a kick that sent it high in the air, he exclaimed: 'Git out of the road, gosh dern you, and let somebody run that knows how.'

"I reckon," said Mr. Lincoln, "that the long-legged Congressman, when he saw the rebel muskets, must have felt a good deal like that young fellow did when he saw the old man's shot-gun."

"FOOLING" THE PEOPLE

Lincoln was a strong believer in the virtue of dealing honestly with the people.

"If you once forfeit the confidence of your fellow-citizens," he said to a caller at the White House, "you can never regain their respect and esteem.

"It is true that you may fool all the people some of the time; you can even fool some of the people all the time; but you can't fool all of the people all the time."

HIS "BROAD" STORIES

Mrs. Rose Linder Wilkinson, who often accompanied her father, Judge Linder, in the days when he rode circuit with Mr. Lincoln, tells the following story:

"At night, as a rule, the lawyers spent awhile in the parlor, and permitted the women who happened to be along to sit with them. But after half an hour or so we would notice it was time for us to leave them. I remember traveling the circuit one season when the young wife of one of the lawyers was with him. The place was so crowded that she and I were made to sleep together. When the time came for banishing us from the parlor, we went up to our room and sat there till bed-time, listening to the roars that followed each ether swiftly while those lawyers down-stairs told stoties and laughed till the rafters rang.

"In the morning Mr. Lincoln said to me: 'Rose, did we disturb your sleep last night?' I answered, 'No, I had no sleep'--which was not entirely true but the retort amused him. Then the young lawyer's wife complained to him that we were not fairly used. We came along with them, young women, and when they were having the best time we were sent away like children to go to bed in the dark.

"'But, Madame,' said Mr. Lincoln, 'you would not enjoy the things we laugh at.' And then he entered into a discussion on what have been termed his 'broad' stories. He deplored the fact that men seemed to remember them longer and with less effort than any others.

"My father said: 'But, Lincoln, I don't remember the "broad" part of your stories so much as I do the moral that is in them,' and it was a thing in which they were all agreed."

SORRY FOR THE HORSES

When President Lincoln heard of the Confederate raid at Fairfax, in which a brigadier-general and a number of valuable horses were captured, he gravely observed:

"Well, I am sorry for the horses."

"Sorry for the horses, Mr. President!" exclaimed the Secretary of War, raising his spectacles and throwing himself back in his chair in astonishment.

"Yes," replied Mr., Lincoln, "I can make a brigadier-general in five minutes, but it is not easy to replace a hundred and ten horses."

COLD MOLASSES WAS SWIFTER.

"Old Pap," as the soldiers called General George H. Thomas, was aggravatingly slow at a time when the President wanted him to "get a move on"; in fact, the gallant "Rock of Chickamauga" was evidently entered in a snail-race.

"Some of my generals are so slow," regretfully remarked Lincoln one day, "that molasses in the coldest days of winter is a race horse compared to them.

"They're brave enough, but somehow or other they get fastened in a fence corner, and can't figure their way out."

THEY DIDN'T BUILD IT

In 1862 a delegation of New York millionaires waited upon President Lincoln to request that he furnish a gunboat for the protection of New York harbor.

Mr. Lincoln, after listening patiently, said: "Gentlemen, the credit of the Government is at a very low ebb; greenbacks are not worth more than forty or fifty cents on the dollar; it is impossible for me, in the present condition of things, to furnish you a gunboat, and, in this condition of things, if I was worth half as much as you, gentlemen, are represented to be, and as badly frightened as you seem to be, I would build a gunboat and give it to the Government."

IT WAS UP-HILL WORK.

Two young men called on the President from Springfield, Illinois. Lincoln shook hands with them, and asked about the crops, the weather, etc.

Finally one of the young men said, "Mother is not well, and she sent me up to inquire of you how the suit about the Wells property is getting on."

Lincoln, in the same even tone with which he had asked the question, said: "Give my best wishes and respects to your mother, and tell her I have so many outside matters to attend to now that I have put that case, and others, in the hands of a lawyer friend of mine, and if you will call on him (giving name and address) he will give you the information you want."

After they had gone, a friend, who was present, said: "Mr. Lincoln, you did not seem to know the young men?"

He laughed and replied: "No, I had never seen them before, and I had to beat around the bush until I found who they were. It was up-hill work, but I topped it at last."

LEE'S SLIM ANIMAL.

President Lincoln wrote to General Hooker on June 5, 1863, warning Hooker not to run any risk of being entangled on the Rappahannock "like an ox jumped half over a fence and liable to be torn by dogs, front and rear, without a fair chance to give one way or kick the other." On the l0th he warned Hooker not to go south of the Rappahannock upon Lee's moving north of it. "I think Lee's army and not Richmond is your true objective power. If he comes toward the upper Potomac, follow on his flank, and on the inside track, shortening your lines while he lengthens his. Fight him, too, when opportunity offers. If he stay where he is, fret him, and fret him."

On the 14th again he says: "So far as we can make out here, the enemy have Milroy surrounded at Winchester, and Tyler at Martinsburg. If they could hold out for a few days, could you help them? If the head of Lee's army is at Martinsburg, and the tail of it on the flank road between Fredericksburg and Chancellorsville, the animal must be very slim somewhere; could you not break him?"

"MRS. NORTH AND HER ATTORNEY."

In the issue of London "Punch" of September 24th, 1864, President Lincoln is pictured as sitting at a table in his law office, while in a chair to his tight is a client, Mrs. North. The latter is a fine client for any attorney to have on his list, being wealthy and liberal, but as the lady is giving her counsel, who has represented her in a legal way for four years, notice that she proposes to put her legal business in the hands of another lawyer, the dejected look upon the face of Attorney Lincoln is easily accounted for. "Punch" puts these words in the lady's mouth:

MRS. NORTH: "You see, Mr. Lincoln, we have failed utterly in our course of action; I want peace, and so, if you cannot effect an amicable arrangement, I must put the case into other hands."

In this cartoon, "Punch" merely reflected the idea, or sentiment, current in England in 1864, that the North was much dissatisfied with the War policy of President Lincoln; and would surely elect General McClellan to succeed the Westerner in the White House. At the election McClellan carried but one Northern State--New Jersey, where he was born--President Lincoln sweeping the country like a prairie fire.

"Punch" had evidently been deceived by some bold, bad man, who wanted a little spending money, and sold the prediction to the funny journal with a certificate of character attached, written by--possibly--a member of the Horse Marines. "Punch," was very much disgusted to find that its credulity and faith in mankind had been so imposed upon, especially when the election returns showed that "the-War-is-a-failure" candidate ran so slowly that Lincoln passed him as easily as though the Democratic nominee was tied to a post.

SATISFACTION TO THE SOUL.

In the far-away days when "Abe" went to school in Indiana, they had exercises, exhibitions and speaking-meetings in the schoolhouse or the church, and "Abe" was the "star." His father was a Democrat, and at that time "Abe" agreed with his parent. He would frequently make political and other speeches to the boys and explain tangled questions.

Booneville was the county seat of Warrick county, situated about fifteen miles from Gentryville. Thither "Abe" walked to be present at the sittings of the court, and listened attentively to the trials and the speeches of the lawyers.

One of the trials was that of a murderer. He was defended by Mr. John Breckinridge, and at the conclusion of his speech "Abe" was so enthusiastic that he ventured to compliment him. Breckinridge looked at the shabby boy, thanked him, and passed on his way.

Many years afterwards, in 1862, Breckinridge called on the President, and he was told, "It was the best speech that I, up to that time, had ever heard. If I could, as I then thought, make as good a speech as that, my soul would be satisfied."

WITHDREW THE COLT.

Mr. Alcott, of Elgin, Ill., tells of seeing Mr. Lincoln coming away from church unusually early one Sunday morning. "The sermon could not have been more than half way through," says Mr. Alcott. "'Tad' was slung across his left arm like a pair of saddlebags, and Mr. Lincoln was striding along with long, deliberate steps toward his home. On one of the street corners he encountered a group of his fellow-townsmen. Mr. Lincoln anticipated the question which was about to be put by the group, and, taking his figure of speech from practices with which they were only too familiar, said: 'Gentlemen, I entered this colt, but he kicked around so I had to withdraw him.'"

"TAD" GOT HIS DOLLAR.

No matter who was with the President, or how intently absorbed, his little son "Tad" was always welcome. He almost always accompanied his father.

Once, on the way to Fortress Monroe, he became very troublesome. The President was much engaged in conversation with the party who accompanied him, and he at length said:

"'Tad,' if you will be a good boy, and not disturb me any more until we get to Fortress Monroe, I will give you a dollar."

The hope of reward was effectual for awhile in securing silence, but, boylike, "Tad" soon forgot his promise, and was as noisy as ever. Upon reaching their destination, however, he said, very promptly: "Father, I want my dollar." Mr. Lincoln looked at him half-reproachfully for an instant, and then, taking from his pocketbook a dollar note, he said "Well, my son, at any rate, I will keep my part of the bargain."

TELLS AN EDITOR ABOUT NASBY.

Henry J. Raymond, the famous New York editor, thus tells of Mr. Lincoln's fondness for the Nasby letters:

"It has been well said by a profound critic of Shakespeare, and it occurs to me as very appropriate in this connection, that the spirit which held the woe of Lear and the tragedy of "Hamlet" would have broken had it not also had the humor of the "Merry Wives of Windsor" and the merriment of the "Midsummer Night's Dream."

"This is as true of Mr. Lincoln as it was of Shakespeare. The capacity to tell and enjoy a good anecdote no doubt prolonged his life.

"The Saturday evening before he left Washington to go to the front, just previous to the capture of Richmond, I was with him from seven o'clock till nearly twelve. It had been one of his most trying days. The pressure of office-seekers was greater at this juncture than I ever knew it to be, and he was almost worn out.

"Among the callers that evening was a party composed of two Senators, a Representative, an ex-Lieutenant-Governor of a Western State, and several private citizens. They had business of great importance, involving the necessity of the President's examination of voluminous documents. Pushing everything aside, he said to one of the party:

"'Have you seen the Nasby papers?'

"'No, I have not,' was the reply; 'who is Nasby?'

"'There is a chap out in Ohio,' returned the President, 'who has been writing a series of letters in the newspapers over the signature of Petroleum V. Nasby. Some one sent me a pamphlet collection of them the other day. I am going to write to "Petroleum" to come down here, and I intend to tell him if he will communicate his talent to me, I will swap places with him!'

"Thereupon he arose, went to a drawer in his desk, and, taking out the 'Letters,' sat down and read one to the company, finding in their enjoyment of it the temporary excitement and relief which another man would have found in a glass of wine. The instant he had ceased, the book was thrown aside, his countenance relapsed into its habitual serious expression, and the business was entered upon with the utmost earnestness."

LONG AND SHORT OF IT.

On the occasion of a serenade, the President was called for by the crowd assembled. He appeared at a window with his wife (who was somewhat below the medium height), and made the following "brief remarks":

"Here I am, and here is Mrs. Lincoln. That's the long and the short of it."

MORE PEGS THAN HOLES.

Some gentlemen were once finding fault with the President because certain generals were not given commands.

"The fact is," replied President Lincoln, "I have got more pegs than I have holes to put them in."

"WEBSTER COULDN'T HAVE DONE MORE."

Lincoln "got even" with the Illinois Central Railroad Company, in 1855, in a most substantial way, at the same time secured sweet revenge for an insult, unwarranted in every way, put upon him by one of the officials of that corporation.

Lincoln and Herndon defended the Illinois Central Railroad in an action brought by McLean County, Illinois, in August, 1853, to recover taxes alleged to be due the county from the road. The Legislature had granted the road immunity from taxation, and this was a case intended to test the constitutionality of the law. The road sent a retainer fee of $250.

In the lower court the case was decided in favor of the railroad. An appeal to the Supreme Court followed, was argued twice, and finally decided in favor of the road. This last decision was rendered some time in 1855. Lincoln then went to Chicago and presented the bill for legal services. Lincoln and Herndon only asked for $2,000 more.

The official to whom he was referred, after looking at the bill, expressed great surprise.

"Why, sir," he exclaimed, "this is as much as Daniel Webster himself would have charged. We cannot allow such a claim."

"Why not?" asked Lincoln.

"We could have hired first-class lawyers at that figure," was the response.

"We won the case, didn't we?" queried Lincoln.

"Certainly," replied the official.

"Daniel Webster, then," retorted Lincoln in no amiable tone, "couldn't have done more," and "Abe" walked out of the official's office.

Lincoln withdrew the bill, and started for home. On the way he stopped at Bloomington, where he met Grant Goodrich, Archibald Williams, Norman B. Judd, O. H. Browning, and other attorneys, who, on learning of his modest charge for the valuable services rendered the railroad, induced him to increase the demand to $5,000, and to bring suit for that sum.

This was done at once. On the trial six lawyers certified that the bill was reasonable, and judgment for that sum went by default; the judgment was promptly paid, and, of course, his partner, Herndon, got "your half Billy," without delay.

LINCOLN MET CLAY.

When a member of Congress, Lincoln went to Lexington, Kentucky, to hear Henry Clay speak. The Westerner, a Kentuckian by birth, and destined to reach the great goal Clay had so often sought, wanted to meet the "Millboy of the Slashes." The address was a tame affair, as was the personal greeting when Lincoln made himself known. Clay was courteous, but cold. He may never have heard of the man, then in his presence, who was to secure, without solicitation, the prize which he for many years had unsuccessfully sought. Lincoln was disenchanted; his ideal was shattered. One reason why Clay had not realized his ambition had become apparent.

Clay was cool and dignified; Lincoln was cordial and hearty. Clay's hand was bloodless and frosty, with no vigorous grip in it; Lincoln's was warm, and its clasp was expressive of kindliness and sympathy.

REMINDED "ABE" OF A LITTLE JOKE

President Lincoln had a little joke at the expense of General George B. McClellan, the Democratic candidate for the Presidency in opposition to the Westerner in 1864. McClellan was nominated by the Democratic National Convention, which assembled at Chicago, but after he had been named, and also during the campaign, the military candidate was characteristically slow in coming to the front.

President Lincoln had his eye upon every move made by General McClellan during the campaign, and when reference was made one day, in his presence, to the deliberation and caution of the New Jerseyite, Mr. Lincoln remarked, with a twinkle in his eye, "Perhaps he is intrenching."

The cartoon we reproduce appeared in "Harper's Weekly," September 17th, 1864, and shows General McClellan, with his little spade in hand, being subjected to the scrutiny of the President--the man who gave McClellan, when the latter was Commander-in-Chief of the Union forces, every opportunity in the world to distinguish himself. There is a smile on the face of "Honest Abe," which shows conclusively that he does not regard his political opponent as likely to prove formidable in any way. President Lincoln "sized up" McClellan in 1861-2, and knew, to a fraction, how much of a man he was, what he could do, and how he went about doing it. McClellan was no politician, while the President was the shrewdest of political diplomats.

HIS DIGNITY SAVED HIM.

When Washington had become an armed camp, and full of soldiers, President Lincoln and his Cabinet officers drove daily to one or another of these camps. Very often his outing for the day was attending some ceremony incident to camp life: a military funeral, a camp wedding, a review, a flag-raising. He did not often make speeches. "I have made a great many poor speeches," he said one day, in excusing himself, "and I now feel relieved that my dignity does not permit me to be a public speaker."

THE MAN HE WAS LOOKNG FOR

Judge Kelly, of Pennsylvania, who was one of the committee to advise Lincoln of his nomination, and who was himself a great many feet high, had been eyeing Lincoln's lofty form with a mixture of admiration and possibly jealousy.

This had not escaped Lincoln, and as he shook hands with the judge he inquired, "What is your height?"

"Six feet three. What is yours, Mr. Lincoln?"

"Six feet four."

"Then," said the judge, "Pennsylvania bows to Illinois. My dear man, for years my heart has been aching for a President that I could look up to, and I've at last found him."

HIS CABINET CHANCES POOR

Mr. Jeriah Bonham, in describing a visit he paid Lincoln at his room in the State House at Springfield, where he found him quite alone, except that two of his children, one of whom was "Tad," were with him.

"The door was open.

"We walked in and were at once recognized and seated--the two boys still continuing their play about the room. "Tad" was spinning his top; and Lincoln, as we entered, had just finished adjusting the string for him so as to give the top the greatest degree of force. He remarked that he was having a little fun with the boys."

At another time, at Lincoln's residence, "Tad" came into the room, and, putting his hand to his mouth, and his mouth to his father's ear, said, in a boy's whisper: "Ma says come to supper."

All heard the announcement; and Lincoln, perceiving this, said: "You have heard, gentlemen, the announcement concerning the interesting state of things in the dining-room. It will never do for me, if elected, to make this young man a member of my Cabinet, for it is plain he cannot be trusted with secrets of state."

THE GENERAL WAS "HEADED IN"

A Union general, operating with his command in West Virginia, allowed himself and his men to be trapped, and it was feared his force would be captured by the Confederates. The President heard the report read by the operator, as it came over the wire, and remarked:

"Once there was a man out West who was 'heading' a barrel, as they used to call it. He worked like a good fellow in driving down the hoops, but just about the time he thought he had the job done, the head would fall in. Then he had to do the work all over again.

"All at once a bright idea entered his brain, and he wondered how it was he hadn't figured it out before. His boy, a bright, smart lad, was standing by, very much interested in the business, and, lifting the young one up, he put him inside the barrel, telling him to hold the head in its proper place, while he pounded down the hoops on the sides. This worked like a charm, and he soon had the 'heading' done.

"Then he realized that his boy was inside the barrel, and how to get him out he couldn't for his life figure out. General Blank is now inside the barrel, 'headed in,' and the job now is to get him out."

SUGAR-COATED

Government Printer Defrees, when one of the President's messages was being printed, was a good deal disturbed by the use of the term "sugar-coated," and finally went to Mr. Lincoln about it.

Their relations to each other being of the most intimate character, he told the President frankly that he ought to remember that a message to Congress was a different affair from a speech at a mass meeting in Illinois; that the messages became a part of history, and should be written accordingly.

"What is the matter now?" inquired the President.

"Why," said Defrees, "you have used an undignified expression in the message"; and, reading the paragraph aloud, he added, "I would alter the structure of that, if I were you."

"Defrees," replied the President, "that word expresses exactly my idea, and I am not going to change it. The time will never come in this country when people won't know exactly what 'sugar-coated' means."

COULD MAKE "RABBIT-TRACKS"

When a grocery clerk at New Salem, the annual election came around. A Mr. Graham was clerk, but his assistant was absent, and it was necessary to find a man to fill his place. Lincoln, a "tall young man," had already concentrated on himself the attention of the people of the town, and Graham easily discovered him. Asking him if he could write, "Abe" modestly replied, "I can make a few rabbit-tracks." His rabbit-tracks proving to be legible and even graceful, he was employed.

The voters soon discovered that the new assistant clerk was honest and fair, and performed his duties satisfactorily, and when, the work done, he began to "entertain them with stories," they found that their town had made a valuable personal and social acquisition.

LINCOLN PROTECTED CURRENCY ISSUES.

Marshal Ward Lamon was in President Lincoln's office in the White House one day, and casually asked the President if he knew how the currency of the country was made. Greenbacks were then under full headway of circulation, these bits of paper being the representatives of United State money.

"Our currency," was the President's answer, "is made, as the lawyers would put it, in their legal way, in the following manner, to-wit: The official engraver strikes off the sheets, passes them over to the Register of the Currency, who, after placing his earmarks upon them, signs the same; the Register turns them over to old Father Spinner, who proceeds to embellish them with his wonderful signature at the bottom; Father Spinner sends them to Secretary of the Treasury Chase, and he, as a final act in the matter, issues them to the public as money--and may the good Lord help any fellow that doesn't take all he can honestly get of them!"

Taking from his pocket a $5 greenback, with a twinkle in his eye, the President then said: "Look at Spinner's signature! Was there ever anything like it on earth? Yet it is unmistakable; no one will ever be able to counterfeit it!"

Lamon then goes on to say:

"'But,' I said, 'you certainly don't suppose that Spinner actually wrote his name on that bill, do you?'

"'Certainly, I do; why not?' queried Mr. Lincoln.

"I then asked, 'How much of this currency have we afloat?'

"He remained thoughtful for a moment, and then stated the amount.

"I continued: 'How many times do you think a man can write a signature like Spinner's in the course of twenty-four hours?'

"The beam of hilarity left the countenance of the President at once. He put the greenback into his vest pocket, and walked the floor; after awhile he stopped, heaved a long breath and said: 'This thing frightens me!' He then rang for a messenger and told him to ask the Secretary of the Treasury to please come over to see him.

"Mr. Chase soon put in an appearance; President Lincoln stated the cause of his alarm, and asked Mr. Chase to explain in detail the operations, methods, system of checks, etc., in his office, and a lengthy discussion followed, President Lincoln contending there were not sufficient safeguards afforded in any degree in the money-making department, and Secretary Chase insisting that every protection was afforded he could devise."

Afterward the President called the attention of Congress to this important question, and devices were adopted whereby a check was put upon the issue of greenbacks that no spurious ones ever came out of the Treasury Department, at least. Counterfeiters were busy, though, but this was not the fault of the Treasury.

IT TICKLED THE LITTLE WOMAN

Lincoln had been in the telegraph office at Springfield during the casting of the first and second ballots in the Republican National Convention at Chicago, and then left and went over to the office of the State Journal, where he was sitting conversing with friends while the third ballot was being taken.

In a few moments came across the wires the announcement of the result. The superintendent of the telegraph company wrote on a scrap of paper: "Mr. Lincoln, you are nominated on the third ballot," and a boy ran with the message to Lincoln.

He looked at it in silence, amid the shouts of those around him; then rising and putting it in his pocket, he said quietly: "There's a little woman down at our house would like to hear this; I'll go down and tell her."

DEAD DOG NO CURE

Lincoln's quarrel with Shields was his last personal encounter. In later years it became his duty to give an official reprimand to a young officer who had been court-martialed for a quarrel with one of his associates. The reprimand is probably the gentlest on record:

"Quarrel not at all. No man resolved to make the most of himself can spare time for personal contention. Still less can he afford to take all the consequences, including the vitiating of his temper and the loss of self-control. Yield larger things to which you can show no more than equal right; and yield lesser ones, though clearly your own.

"Better give your path to a dog than be bitten by him in contesting for the right. Even killing the dog would not cure the bite."

"THOROUGH" IS A GOOD WORD

Some one came to the President with a story about a plot to accomplish some mischief in the Government. Lincoln listened to what was a very superficial and ill-formed story, and then said: "There is one thing that I have learned, and that you have not. It is only one word--'thorough.'"

Then, bringing his hand down on the table with a thump to emphasize his meaning, he added, "thorough!"

THE CABINET WAS A-SETTIN'

Being in Washington one day, the Rev. Robert Collyer thought he'd take a look around. In passing through the grounds surrounding the White House, he cast a glance toward the Presidential residence, and was astonished to see three pairs of feet resting on the ledge of an open window in one of the apartments of the second story. The divine paused for a moment, calmly surveyed the unique spectacle, and then resumed his walk toward the War Department.

Seeing a laborer at work not far from the Executive Mansion, Mr. Collyer asked him what it all meant. To whom did the feet belong, and, particularly, the mammoth ones? "You old fool," answered the workman, "that's the Cabinet, which is a-settin', an' them thar big feet belongs to 'Old Abe.'"

A BULLET THROUGH HIS HAT

A soldier tells the following story of an attempt upon the life of Mr. Lincoln "One night I was doing sentinel duty at the entrance to the Soldiers' Home. This was about the middle of August, 1864. About eleven o'clock I heard a rifle shot, in the direction of the city, and shortly afterwards I heard approaching hoof-beats. In two or three minutes a horse came dashing up. I recognized the belated President. The President was bareheaded. The President simply thought that his horse had taken fright at the discharge of the firearms.

"On going back to the place where the shot had been heard, we found the President's hat. It was a plain silk hat, and upon examination we discovered a bullet hole through the crown.

"The next day, upon receiving the hat, the President remarked that it was made by some foolish marksman, and was not intended for him; but added that he wished nothing said about the matter.

"The President said, philosophically: 'I long ago made up my mind that if anybody wants to kill me, he will do it. Besides, in this case, it seems to me, the man who would succeed me would be just as objectionable to my enemies--if I have any.'

"One dark night, as he was going out with a friend, he took along a heavy cane, remarking, good-naturedly: 'Mother (Mrs. Lincoln) has got a notion into her head that I shall be assassinated, and to please her I take a cane when I go over to the War Department at night--when I don't forget it.'"

NO KIND TO GET TO HEAVEN ON

Two ladies from Tennessee called at the White House one day and begged Mr. Lincoln to release their husbands, who were rebel prisoners at Johnson's Island. One of the fair petitioners urged as a reason for the liberation of her husband that he was a very religious man, and rang the changes on this pious plea.

"Madam," said Mr. Lincoln, "you say your husband is a religious man. Perhaps I am not a good judge of such matters, but in my opinion the religion that makes men rebel and fight against their government is not the genuine article; nor is the religion the right sort which reconciles them to the idea of eating their bread in the sweat of other men's faces. It is not the kind to get to heaven on."

Later, however, the order of release was made, President Lincoln remarking, with impressive solemnity, that he would expect the ladies to subdue the rebellious spirit of their husbands, and to that end he thought it would be well to reform their religion. "True patriotism," said he, "is better than the wrong kind of piety."

THE QUESTION OF LEGS

Whenever the people of Lincoln's neighborhood engaged in dispute; whenever a bet was to be decided; when they differed on points of religion or politics; when they wanted to get out of trouble, or desired advice regarding anything on the earth, below it, above it, or under the sea, they went to "Abe."

Two fellows, after a hot dispute lasting some hours, over the problem as to how long a man's legs should be in proportion to the size of his body, stamped into Lincoln's office one day and put the question to him.

Lincoln listened gravely to the arguments advanced by both contestants, spent some time in "reflecting" upon the matter, and then, turning around in his chair and facing the disputants, delivered his opinion with all the gravity of a judge sentencing a fellow-being to death.

"This question has been a source of controversy," he said, slowly and deliberately, "for untold ages, and it is about time it should be definitely decided. It has led to bloodshed in the past, and there is no reason to suppose it will not lead to the same in the future.

"After much thought and consideration, not to mention mental worry and anxiety, it is my opinion, all side issues being swept aside, that a man's lower limbs, in order to preserve harmony of proportion, should be at least long enough to reach from his body to the ground."

GOD NEEDED THAT CHURCH

In the early stages of the war, after several battles had been fought, Union troops seized a church in Alexandria, Va., and used it as a hospital.

A prominent lady of the congregation went to Washington to see Mr. Lincoln and try to get an order for its release.

"Have you applied to the surgeon in charge at Alexandria?" inquired Mr. Lincoln.

"Yes, sir" but I can do nothing with him," was the reply.

"Well, madam," said Mr. Lincoln, "that is an end of it, then. We put him there to attend to just such business, and it is reasonable to suppose that he knows better what should be done under the circumstances than I do."

The lady's face showed her keen disappointment. In order to learn her sentiment, Mr. Lincoln asked:

"How much would you be willing to subscribe toward building a hospital there?"

She said that the war had depreciated Southern property so much that she could afford to give but little.

"This war is not over yet," said Mr. Lincoln, "and there will likely be another fight very soon. That church may be very useful in which to house our wounded soldiers. It is my candid opinion that God needs that church for our wounded fellows; so, madam, I can do nothing for you."

COULDN'T LET GO THE HOG

When Governor Curtin of Pennsylvania described the terrible butchery at the battle of Fredericksburg, Mr. Lincoln was almost broken-hearted.

The Governor regretted that his description had so sadly affected the President. He remarked: "I would give all I possess to know how to rescue you from this terrible war." Then Mr. Lincoln's wonderful recuperative powers asserted themselves and this marvelous man was himself.

Lincoln's whole aspect suddenly changed, and he relieved his mind by telling a story.

"This reminds me, Governor," he said, "of an old farmer out in Illinois that I used to know.

"He took it into his head to go into hog-raising. He sent out to Europe and imported the finest breed of hogs he could buy.

"The prize hog was put in a pen, and the farmer's two mischievous boys, James and John, were told to be sure not to let it out. But James, the worst of the two, let the brute out the next day. The hog went straight for the boys, and drove John up a tree, then the hog went for the seat of James' trousers, and the only way the boy could save himself was by holding on to the hog's tail.

"The hog would not give up his hunt, nor the boy his hold! After they had made a good many circles around the tree, the boy's courage began to give out, and he shouted to his brother, 'I say, John, come down, quick, and help me let go this hog!'

"Now, Governor, that is exactly my case. I wish some one would come and help me to let the hog go."

THE CABINET LINCOLN WANTED

Judge Joseph Gillespie, of Chicago, was a firm friend of Mr. Lincoln, and went to Springfield to see him shortly before his departure for the inauguration.

"It was," said judge Gillespie, "Lincoln's Gethsemane. He feared he was not the man for the great position and the great events which confronted him. Untried in national affairs, unversed in international diplomacy, unacquainted with the men who were foremost in the politics of the nation, he groaned when he saw the inevitable War of the Rebellion coming on. It was in humility of spirit that he told me he believed that the American people had made a mistake in selecting him.

"In the course of our conversation he told me if he could select his cabinet from the old bar that had traveled the circuit with him in the early days, he believed he could avoid war or settle it without a battle, even after the fact of secession.

"'But, Mr. Lincoln,' said I, 'those old lawyers are all Democrats.'

"'I know it,' was his reply. 'But I would rather have Democrats whom I know than Republicans I don't know.'"

IF THEY'D ONLY "SKIP"

General Creswell called at the White House to see the President the day of the latter's assassination. An old friend, serving in the Confederate ranks, had been captured by the Union troops and sent to prison. He had drawn an affidavit setting forth what he knew about the man, particularly mentioning extenuating circumstances.

Creswell found the President very happy. He was greeted with: "Creswell, old fellow, everything is bright this morning. The War is over. It has been a tough time, but we have lived it out,--or some of us have," and he dropped his voice a little on the last clause of the sentence. "But it is over; we are going to have good times now, and a united country."

General Creswell told his story, read his affidavit, and said, "I know the man has acted like a fool, but he is my friend, and a good fellow; let him out; give him to me, and I will be responsible that he won't have anything more to do with the rebs."

"Creswell," replied Mr. Lincoln, "you make me think of a lot of young folks who once started out Maying. To reach their destination, they had to cross a shallow stream, and did so by means of an old flatboat. When the time came to return, they found to their dismay that the old scow had disappeared. They were in sore trouble, and thought over all manner of devices for getting over the water, but without avail.

"After a time, one of the boys proposed that each fellow should pick up the girl he liked best and wade over with her. The masterly proposition was carried out, until all that were left upon the island was a little short chap and a great, long, gothic-built, elderly lady.

"Now, Creswell, you are trying to leave me in the same predicament. You fellows are all getting your own friends out of this scrape; and you will succeed in carrying off one after another, until nobody but

Jeff Davis and myself will be left on the island, and then I won't know what to do. How should I feel? How should I look, lugging him over?

"I guess the way to avoid such an embarrassing situation is to let them all out at once."

He made a somewhat similar illustration at an informal Cabinet meeting, at which the disposition of Jefferson Davis and other prominent Confederates was discussed. Each member of the Cabinet gave his opinion; most of them were for hanging the traitors, or for some severe punishment. President Lincoln said nothing.

Finally, Joshua F. Speed, his old and confidential friend, who had been invited to the meeting, said, "I have heard the opinion of your Ministers, and would like to hear yours."

"Well, Josh," replied President Lincoln, "when I was a boy in Indiana, I went to a neighbor's house one morning and found a boy of my own size holding a coon by a string. I asked him what he had and what he was doing.

"He says, 'It's a coon. Dad cotched six last night, and killed all but this poor little cuss. Dad told me to hold him until he came back, and I'm afraid he's going to kill this one too; and oh, "Abe," I do wish he would get away!'

"'Well, why don't you let him loose?'

"'That wouldn't be right; and if I let him go, Dad would give me h--. But if he got away himself, it would be all right.'

"Now," said the President, "if Jeff Davis and those other fellows will only get away, it will be all right. But if we should catch them, and I should let them go, 'Dad would give me h--!'"

"ONE WAR AT A TIME"

Nothing in Lincoln's entire career better illustrated the surprising resources of his mind than his manner of dealing with "The Trent Affair." The readiness and ability with which he met this perilous emergency, in a field entirely new to his experience, was worthy the most accomplished diplomat and statesman. Admirable, also, was his cool courage and self-reliance in following a course radically opposed to the prevailing sentiment throughout the country and in Congress, and contrary to the advice of his own Cabinet.

Secretary of the Navy Welles hastened to approve officially the act of Captain Wilkes in apprehending the Confederate Commissioners Mason and Slidell, Secretary Stanton publicly applauded, and even Secretary of State Seward, whose long public career had made him especially conservative, stated that he was opposed to any concession or surrender of Mason and Slidell.

But Lincoln, with great sagacity, simply said, "One war at a time."

"STRETCHED THE FACTS"

George B. Lincoln, a prominent merchant of Brooklyn, was traveling through the West in 1855-56, and found himself one night in a town on the Illinois River, by the name of Naples. The only tavern of the place had evidently been constructed with reference to business on a small scale. Poor as the prospect seemed, Mr. Lincoln had no alternative but to put up at the place.

The supper-room was also used as a lodging-room. Mr. Lincoln told his host that he thought he would "go to bed."

"Bed!" echoed the landlord. "There is no bed for you in this house unless you sleep with that man yonder. He has the only one we have to spare."

"Well," returned Mr. Lincoln, "the gentleman has possession, and perhaps would not like a bed-fellow."

Upon this a grizzly head appeared out of the pillows, and said:

"What is your name?"

"They call me Lincoln at home," was the reply.

"Lincoln!" repeated the stranger; "any connection of our Illinois Abraham?"

"No," replied Mr. Lincoln. "I fear not."

"Well," said the old gentleman, "I will let any man by the name of 'Lincoln' sleep with me, just for the sake of the name. You have heard of Abe?" he inquired.

"Oh, yes, very often," replied Mr. Lincoln. "No man could travel far in this State without hearing of him, and I would be very glad to claim connection if I could do so honestly."

"Well," said the old gentleman, "my name is Simmons. 'Abe' and I used to live and work together when young men. Many a job of woodcutting and rail-splitting have I done up with him. Abe Lincoln was the likeliest boy in God's world. He would work all day as hard as any of us and study by firelight in the loghouse half the night; and in this way he made himself a thorough, practical surveyor. Once, during those days, I was in the upper part of the State, and I met General Ewing, whom President Jackson had sent to the Northwest to make surveys. I told him about Abe Lincoln, what a student he was, and that I wanted he should give him a job. He looked over his memorandum, and, holding out a paper, said:

"'There is County must be surveyed; if your friend can do the work properly, I shall be glad to have him undertake it--the compensation will be six hundred dollars.'

"Pleased as I could be, I hastened to Abe, after I got home, with an account of what I had secured for him. He was sitting before the fire in the log-cabin when I told him; and what do you think was his answer? When I finished, he looked up very quietly, and said:

"'Mr. Simmons, I thank you very sincerely for your kindness, but I don't think I will undertake the job.'

"'In the name of wonder,' said I, 'why? Six hundred does not grow upon every bush out here in Illinois.'

"'I know that,' said Abe, 'and I need the money bad enough, Simmons, as you know; but I have never been under obligation to a Democratic Administration, and I never intend to be so long as I can get my living another way. General Ewing must find another man to do his work.'"

A friend related this story to the President one day, and asked him if it were true.

"Pollard Simmons!" said Lincoln. "Well do I remember him. It is correct about our working together, but the old man must have stretched the facts somewhat about the survey of the county. I think I should have been very glad of the job at the time, no matter what Administration was in power."

RAN AWAY WHEN VICTORIOUS.

Three or four days after the battle of Bull Run, some gentlemen who had been on the field called upon the President.

He inquired very minutely regarding all the circumstances of the affair, and, after listening with the utmost attention, said, with a touch of humor: "So it is your notion that we whipped the rebels and then ran away from them!"

WANTED STANTON SPANKED

Old Dennis Hanks was sent to Washington at one time by persons interested in securing the release from jail of several men accused of being copperheads. It was thought Old Dennis might have some influence with the President.

The latter heard Dennis' story and then said: "I will send for Mr. Stanton. It is his business."

Secretary Stanton came into the room, stormed up and down, and said the men ought to be punished more than they were. Mr. Lincoln sat quietly in his chair and waited for the tempest to subside, and then quietly said to Stanton he would like to have the papers next day.

When he had gone, Dennis said:

"'Abe,' if I was as big and as ugly as you are, I would take him over my knee and spank him."

The President replied: "No, Stanton is an able and valuable man for this Nation, and I am glad to bear his anger for the service he can give the Nation."

STANTON WAS OUT OF TOWN.

The quaint remark of the President to an applicant, "My dear sir, I have not much influence with the Administration," was one of Lincoln's little jokes.

Mr. Stanton, Secretary of War, once replied to an order from the President to give a colonel a commission in place of the resigning brigadier:

"I shan't do it, sir! I shan't do it! It isn't the way to do it, sir, and I shan't do it. I don't propose to argue the question with you, sir."

A few days after, the friend of the applicant who had presented the order to Secretary Stanton called upon the President and related his reception. A look of vexation came over the face of the President, and he seemed unwilling to talk of it, and desired the friend to see him another day. He did so, when he gave his visitor a positive order for the promotion. The latter told him he would not speak to Secretary Stanton again until he apologized.

"Oh," said the President, "Stanton has gone to Fortress Monroe, and Dana is acting. He will attend to it for you."

This he said with a manner of relief, as if it was a piece of good luck to find a man there who would obey his orders.

The nomination was sent to the Senate and confirmed.

OFFICE SEEKERS WORSE THAN WAR

When the Republican party came into power, Washington swarmed with office-seekers. They overran the White House and gave the President great annoyance. The incongruity of a man in his position, and with the very life of the country at stake, pausing to appoint postmasters, struck Mr. Lincoln forcibly. "What is the matter, Mr. Lincoln," said a friend one day, when he saw him looking particularly grave and dispirited. "Has anything gone wrong at the front?" "No," said the President, with a tired smile. "It isn't the war; it's the post office at Brownsville, Missouri."

JUSTICE vs. NUMBERS

Lincoln was constantly bothered by members of delegations of "goody-goodies," who knew all about running the War, but had no inside information as to what was going on. Yet, they poured out their advice in streams, until the President was heartily sick of the whole business, and wished the War would find some way to kill off these nuisances.

"How many men have the Confederates now in the field?" asked one of these bores one day.

"About one million two hundred thousand," replied the President.

"Oh, my! Not so many as that, surely, Mr. Lincoln."

"They have fully twelve hundred thousand, no doubt of it. You see, all of our generals when they get whipped say the enemy outnumbers them from three or five to one, and I must believe them. We have four hundred thousand men in the field, and three times four make twelve,-- don't you see it? It is as plain to be seen as the nose on a man's face; and at the rate things are now going, with the great amount of speculation and the small crop of fighting, it will take a long time to overcome twelve hundred thousand rebels in arms.

"If they can get subsistence they have everything else, except a just cause. Yet it is said that 'thrice is he armed that hath his quarrel just.' I am willing, however, to risk our advantage of thrice in justice against their thrice in numbers."

NO FALSE PRIDE IN LINCOLN

General McClellan had little or no conception of the greatness of Abraham Lincoln. As time went on, he began to show plainly his contempt of the President, frequently allowing him to wait in the ante-room of his house while he transacted business with others. This discourtesy was so open that McClellan's staff noticed it, and newspaper correspondents commented on it. The President was too keen not to see the situation, but he was strong enough to ignore it. It was a battle he wanted from McClellan, not deference.

"I will hold McClellan's horse, if he will only bring us success," he said one day.

EXTRA MEMBER OF THE CABINET

G. H. Giddings was selected as the bearer of a message from the President to Governor Sam Houston, of Texas. A conflict had arisen there between the Southern party and the Governor, Sam Houston, and on March 18 the latter had been deposed. When Mr. Lincoln heard of this, he decided to try to get a message to the Governor, offering United States support if he would put himself at the head of the Union party of the State.

Mr. Giddings thus told of his interview with the President:

"He said to me that the message was of such importance that, before handing it to me, he would read it to me. Before beginning to read he said, 'This is a confidential and secret message. No one besides my Cabinet and myself knows anything about it, and we are all sworn to secrecy. I am going to swear you in as one of my Cabinet.'

"And then he said to me in a jocular way, 'Hold up your right hand,' which I did.

"'Now,' said he, consider yourself a member of my Cabinet.'"

SLEEP STANDING UP

McClellan was a thorn in Lincoln's side--"always up in the air," as the President put it--and yet he hesitated to remove him. "The Young Napoleon" was a good organizer, but no fighter. Lincoln sent him everything necessary in the way of men, ammunition, artillery and equipments, but he was forever unready.

Instead of making a forward movement at the time expected, he would notify the President that he must have more men. These were given him as rapidly as possible, and then would come a demand for more horses, more this and that, usually winding up with a demand for still "more men."

Lincoln bore it all in patience for a long time, but one day, when he had received another request for more men, he made a vigorous protest.

"If I gave McClellan all the men he asks for," said the President, "they couldn't find room to lie down. They'd have to sleep standing up."

LINCOLN SILENCES SEWARD

General Farnsworth told the writer nearly twenty years ago that, being in the War Office one day, Secretary Stanton told him that at the last Cabinet meeting he had learned a lesson he should never forget, and thought he had obtained an insight into Mr. Lincoln's wonderful power over the masses. The Secretary said a Cabinet meeting was called to consider our relations with England in regard to the Mason-Slidell affair. One after another of the Cabinet presented his views, and Mr. Seward read an elaborate diplomatic dispatch, which he had prepared.

Finally Mr. Lincoln read what he termed "a few brief remarks upon the subject," and asked the opinions of his auditors. They unanimously agreed that our side of the question needed no more argument than was contained in the President's "few brief remarks."

Mr. Seward said he would be glad to adopt the remarks, and, giving them more of the phraseology usual in diplomatic circles, send them to Lord Palmerston, the British premier.

"Then," said Secretary Stanton, "came the demonstration. The President, half wheeling in his seat, threw one leg over the chair-arm, and, holding the letter in his hand, said, 'Seward, do you suppose Palmerston will understand our position from that letter, just as it is?'

"'Certainly, Mr. President.'

"'Do you suppcse the London Times will?'

"'Certainly.'

"'Do you suppose the average Englishman of affairs will?'

"'Certainly; it cannot be mistaken in England.'

"'Do you suppose that a hackman out on his box (pointing to the street) will understand it?'

"'Very readily, Mr. President.'

"'Very well, Seward, I guess we'll let her slide just as she is.'

"And the letter did 'slide,' and settled the whole business in a manner that was effective."

A VERY BRAINY NUBBIN

President Lincoln and Secretary of State Seward met Alexander H. Stephens, Vice-President of the Confederacy, on February 2nd, 1865, on the River Queen, at Fortress Monroe. Stephens was enveloped in overcoats and shawls, and had the appearance of a fair-sized man. He began to take off one wrapping after another, until the small, shriveled old man stood before them.

Lincoln quietly said to Seward: "This is the largest shucking for so small a nubbin that I ever saw."

President Lincoln had a friendly conference, but presented his ultimatum that the one and only condition of peace was that Confederates "must cease their resistance."

DIDN'T WANT A MILITARY REPUTATION

Lincoln was averse to being put up as a military hero.

When General Cass was a candidate for the Presidency his friends sought to endow him with a military reputation.

Lincoln, at that time a representative in Congress, delivered a speech before the House, which, in its allusion to Mr. Cass, was exquisitely sarcastic and irresistibly humorous:

"By the way, Mr. Speaker," said Lincoln, "do you know I am a military hero?

"Yes, sir, in the days of the Black Hawk War, I fought, bled, and came away.

"Speaking of General Cass's career reminds me of my own.

"I was not at Stillman's defeat, but I was about as near it as Cass to Hull's surrender; and like him I saw the place very soon afterwards.

"It is quite certain I did not break my sword, for I had none to break, but I bent my musket pretty badly on one occasion.

"If General Cass went in advance of me picking whortleberries, I guess I surpassed him in charging upon the wild onion.

"If he saw any live, fighting Indians, it was more than I did, but I had a good many bloody struggles with the mosquitoes, and although I never fainted from loss of blood, I can truly say that I was often very hungry."

Lincoln concluded by saying that if he ever turned Democrat and should run for the Presidency, he hoped they would not make fun of him by attempting to make him a military hero.

LINCOLN'S IDEAS ON CROSSING A RIVER WHEN HE GOT TO IT

Lincoln's reply to a Springfield (Illinois) clergyman, who asked him what was to be his policy on the slavery question was most apt:

"Well, your question is rather a cool one, but I will answer it by telling you a story:

"You know Father B., the old Methodist preacher? and you know Fox River and its freshets?

"Well, once in the presence of Father B., a young Methodist was worrying about Fox River, and expressing fears that he should be prevented from fulfilling some of his appointments by a freshet in the river.

"Father B. checked him in his gravest manner. Said he:

"'Young man, I have always made it a rule in my life not to cross Fox River till I get to it.'

"And," said the President, "I am not going to worry myself over the slavery question till I get to it."

A few days afterward a Methodist minister called on the President, and on being presented to him, said, simply:

"Mr. President, I have come to tell you that I think we have got to Fox River!"

Lincoln thanked the clergyman, and laughed heartily.

PRESIDENT NOMINATED FIRST.

The day of Lincoln's second nomination for the Presidency he forgot all about the Republican National Convention, sitting at Baltimore, and wandered over to the War Department. While there, a telegram came announcing the nomination of Johnson as Vice-President.

"What," said Lincoln to the operator, "do they nominate a Vice-President before they do a President?"

"Why," replied the astonished official, "have you not heard of your own nomination? It was sent to the White House two hours ago."

"It is all right," replied the President; "I shall probably find it on my return."

HIS PASSES TO RICHMOND NOT HONORED

A man called upon the President and solicited a pass for Richmond.

"Well," said the President, "I would be very happy to oblige, if my passes were respected; but the fact is, sir, I have, within the past two years, given passes to two hundred and fifty thousand men to go to Richmond, and not one has got there yet."

The applicant quietly and respectfully withdrew on his tiptoes.

"PUBLIC HANGMAN" FOR THE UNITED STATES

A certain United States Senator, who believed that every man who believed in secession should be hanged, asked the President what he intended to do when the War was over.

"Reconstruct the machinery of this Government," quickly replied Lincoln.

"You are certainly crazy," was the Senator's heated response. "You talk as if treason was not henceforth to be made odious, but that the traitors, cutthroats and authors of this War should not only go unpunished, but receive encouragement to repeat their treason with impunity! They should be hanged higher than Haman, sir! Yes, higher than any malefactor the world has ever known!"

The President was entirely unmoved, but, after a moment's pause, put a question which all but drove his visitor insane.

"Now, Senator, suppose that when this hanging arrangement has been agreed upon, you accept the post of Chief Executioner. If you will take the office, I will make you a brigadier general and Public Hangman for the United States. That would just about suit you, wouldn't it?"

"I am a gentleman, sir," returned the Senator, "and I certainly thought you knew me better than to believe me capable of doing such dirty work. You are jesting, Mr. President."

The President was extremely patient, exhibiting no signs of ire, and to this bit of temper on the part of the Senator responded:

"You speak of being a gentleman; yet you forget that in this free country all men are equal, the vagrant and the gentleman standing on the same ground when it comes to rights and duties, particularly in time of war. Therefore, being a gentleman, as you claim, and a law-abiding citizen, I trust, you are not exempt from doing even the dirty work at which your high spirit revolts."

This was too much for the Senator, who quitted the room abruptly, and never again showed his face in the White House while Lincoln occupied it.

"He won't bother me again," was the President's remark as he departed.

FEW, BUT BOISTEROUS

Lincoln was a very quiet man, and went about his business in a quiet way, making the least noise possible. He heartily disliked those boisterous people who were constantly deluging him with advice, and shouting at the tops of their voices whenever they appeared at the White House. "These noisy people create a great clamor," said he one day, in conversation with some personal friends, "and remind me, by the way, of a good story I heard out in Illinois while I was practicing, or trying to practice, some law there. I will say, though, that I practiced more law than I ever got paid for.

"A fellow who lived just out of town, on the bank of a large marsh, conceived a big idea in the money-making line. He took it to a prominent merchant, and began to develop his plans and specifications. 'There are at least ten million frogs in that marsh near me, an' I'll just arrest a couple of carloads of them and hand them over to you. You can send them to the big cities and make lots of money for both of us. Frogs' legs are great delicacies in the big towns, an' not very plentiful. It won't take me more'n two or three days to pick 'em. They make so much noise my family can't sleep, and by this deal I'll get rid of a nuisance and gather in some cash.'

"The merchant agreed to the proposition, promised the fellow he would pay him well for the two carloads. Two days passed, then three, and finally two weeks were gone before the fellow showed up again, carrying a small basket. He looked weary and 'done up,' and he wasn't talkative a bit. He threw the basket on the counter with the remark, 'There's your frogs.'

"'You haven't two carloads in that basket, have you?' inquired the merchant.

"'No,' was the reply, 'and there ain't no two carloads in all this blasted world.'

"'I thought you said there were at least ten millions of 'em in that marsh near you, according to the noise they made,' observed the merchant. 'Your people couldn't sleep because of 'em.'

"'Well,' said the fellow, 'accordin' to the noise they made, there was, I thought, a hundred million of 'em, but when I had waded and swum that there marsh day and night fer two blessed weeks, I couldn't harvest but six. There's two or three left yet, an' the marsh is as noisy as it uster be. We haven't catched up on any of our lost sleep yet. Now, you can have these here six, an' I won't charge you a cent fer 'em.'

"You can see by this little yarn," remarked the President, "that these boisterous people make too much noise in proportion to their numbers."

KEEP PEGGING AWAY

Being asked one time by an "anxious" visitor as to what he would do in certain contingencies--provided the rebellion was not subdued after three or four years of effort on the part of the Government

"Oh," replied the President, "there is no alternative but to keep 'pegging' away!"

BEWARE OF THE TAIL

After the issue of the Emancipation Proclamation, Governor Morgan, of New York, was at the White House one day, when the President said:

"I do not agree with those who say that slavery is dead. We are like whalers who have been long on a chase--we have at last got the harpoon into the monster, but we must now look how we steer, or, with one 'flop' of his tail, he will yet send us all into eternity!"

THERE WAS NO NEED OF A STORY

Dr. Hovey, of Dansville, New York, thought he would call and see the President.

Upon arriving at the White House he found the President on horseback, ready for a start.

Approaching him, he said:

"President Lincoln, I thought I would call and see you before leaving the city, and hear you tell a story."

The President greeted him pleasantly, and asked where he was from.

"From Western New York."

"Well, that's a good enough country without stories," replied the President, and off he rode.

FORGOT EVERYTHING HE KNEW BEFORE

President Lincoln, while entertaining a few select friends, is said to have related the following anecdote of a man who knew too much:

He was a careful, painstaking fellow, who always wanted to be absolutely exact, and as a result he frequently got the ill-will of his less careful superiors.

During the administration of President Jackson there was a singular young gentleman employed in the Public Postoffice in Washington.

His name was G.; he was from Tennessee, the son of a widow, a neighbor of the President, on which account the old hero had a kind feeling for him, and always got him out of difficulties with some of the higher officials, to whom his singular interference was distasteful.

Among other things, it is said of him that while employed in the General Post Office, on one occasion he had to copy a letter to Major H., a high official, in answer to an application made by an old gentleman in Virginia or Pennsylvania, for the establishment of a new post office.

The writer of the letter said the application could not be granted, in consequence of the applicant's "proximity" to another office.

When the letter came into G.'s hand to copy, being a great stickler for plainness, he altered "proximity" to "nearness to."

Major H. observed it, and asked G. why he altered his letter.

"Why," replied G., "because I don't think the man would understand what you mean by proximity."

"Well," said Major H., "try him; put in the 'proximity' again."

In a few days a letter was received from the applicant, in which he very indignantly said that his father had fought for liberty in the second war for independence, and he should like to have the name of the scoundrel who brought the charge of proximity or anything else wrong against him.

"There," said G., "did I not say so?"

G. carried his improvements so far that Mr. Berry, the Postmaster-General, said to him: "I don't want you any longer; you know too much."

Poor G. went out, but his old friend got him another place.

This time G.'s ideas underwent a change. He was one day very busy writing, when a stranger called in and asked him where the Patent Office was.

"I don't know," said G.

"Can you tell me where the Treasury Department is?" said the stranger. "No," said G.

'Nor the President's house?"

"No."

The stranger finally asked him if he knew where the Capitol was.

"No," replied G.

"Do you live in Washington, sir?"

"Yes, sir," said G.

"Good Lord! and don't you know where the Patent Office, Treasury, President's house and Capitol are?"

"Stranger," said G., "I was turned out of the post office for knowing too much. I don't mean to offend in that way again.

"I am paid for keeping this book.

"I believe I know that much; but if you find me knowing anything more you may take my head."

"Good morning," said the stranger.

WHAT AILED THE BOYS

Mr. Roland Diller, who was one of Mr. Lincoln's neighbors in Springfield, tells the following:

"I was called to the door one day by the cries of children in the street, and there was Mr. Lincoln, striding by with two of his boys, both of whom were wailing aloud. 'Why, Mr. Lincoln, what's the matter with the boys?' I asked.

"'Just what's the matter with the whole world,' Lincoln replied. 'I've got three walnuts, and each wants two.'"

ANGELS COULDN'T SWEAR IT RIGHT

The President was once speaking about an attack made on him by the Congressional Committee on the Conduct of the War for a certain alleged blunder in the Southwest--the matter involved being one which had fallen directly under the observation of the army officer to whom he was talking, who possessed official evidence completely upsetting all the conclusions of the Committee.

"Might it not be well for me," queried the officer, "to set this matter right in a letter to some paper, stating the facts as they actually transpired?"

"Oh, no," replied the President, "at least, not now. If I were to try to read, much less answer, all the attacks made on me, this shop might as well be closed for any other business. I do the very best I know how the very best I can; and I mean to keep doing so until the end. If the end brings me out all right, what is said against me won't amount to anything. If the end brings me out wrong, ten thousand angels swearing I was right would make no difference."

DON'T TRUST TOO FAIL

In the campaign of 1852, Lincoln, in reply to Douglas' speech, wherein he spoke of confidence in Providence, replied: "Let us stand by our candidate (General Scott) as faithfully as he has always stood by our country, and I much doubt if we do not perceive a slight abatement of Judge Douglas' confidence in Providence as well as the people. I suspect that confidence is not more firmly fixed with the judge than it was with the old woman whose horse ran away with her in a buggy. She said she 'trusted in Providence till the britchen broke,' and then she 'didn't know what in airth to do.'"

"MAJOR GENERAL, I RECKON"

At one time the President had the appointment of a large additional number of brigadier and major generals. Among the immense number of applications, Mr. Lincoln came upon one wherein the claims of a certain worthy (not in the service at all), "for a generalship" were glowingly set forth. But the applicant didn't specify whether he wanted to be brigadier or major general.

The President observed this difficulty, and solved it by a lucid indorsement. The clerk, on receiving the paper again, found written across its back, "Major General, I reckon. A. Lincoln."

WOULD SEE THE TRACKS

Judge Herndon, Lincoln's law partner, said that he never saw Lincoln more cheerful than on the day previous to his departure from Springfield for Washington, and Judge Gillespie, who visited him a few days earlier, found him in excellent spirits.

"I told him that I believed it would do him good to get down to Washington," said Herndon.

"I know it will," Lincoln replied. "I only wish I could have got there to lock the door before the horse was stolen. But when I get to the spot, I can find the tracks."

THE SAME OLD RUM

One of President Lincoln's friends, visiting at the White House, was finding considerable fault with the constant agitation in Congress of the slavery question. He remarked that, after the adoption of the Emancipation policy, he had hoped for something new.

"There was a man down in Maine," said the President, in reply, "who kept a grocery store, and a lot of fellows used to loaf around for their toddy. He only gave 'em New England rum, and they drank pretty considerable of it. But after awhile they began to get tired of that, and kept asking for something new-- something new--all the time. Well, one night, when the whole crowd were around, the grocer brought out his glasses, and says he, 'I've got something New for you to drink, boys, now.'

"'Honor bright?' said they.

"'Honor bright,' says he, and with that he sets out a jug. 'Thar' says he, 'that's something new; it's New England rum!' says he.

"Now," remarked the President, in conclusion, "I guess we're a good deal like that crowd, and Congress is a good deal like that storekeeper!"

IT WAS A FINE FIZZLE

President Lincoln, in company with General Grant, was inspecting the Dutch Gap Canal at City Point. "Grant, do you know what this reminds me of? Out in Springfield, Ill., there was a blacksmith who, not having much to do, took a piece of soft iron and attempted to weld it into an agricultural implement, but discovered that the iron would not hold out; then he concluded it would make a claw hammer; but having too much iron, attempted to make an ax, but decided after working awhile that there was not enough iron left. Finally, becoming disgusted, he filled the forge full of coal and brought the iron to a white heat; then with his tongs he lifted it from the bed of coals, and thrusting it into a tub of water near by, exclaimed: 'Well, if I can't make anything else of you, I will make a fizzle, anyhow.'" "I was afraid that was about what we had done with the Dutch Gap Canal," said General Grant.

TOM CORWINS'S LATEST STORY

One of Mr. Lincoln's warm friends was Dr. Robert Boal, of Lacon, Illinois. Telling of a visit he paid to the White House soon after Mr. Lincoln's inauguration, he said: "I found him the same Lincoln as a struggling lawyer and politician that I did in Washington as President of the United States, yet there was a dignity and self-possession about him in his high official authority. I paid him a second call in the evening. He had thrown off his reserve somewhat, and would walk up and down the room with his hands to his sides and laugh at the joke he was telling, or at one that was told to him. I remember one story he told to me on this occasion.

"Tom Corwin, of Ohio, had been down to Alexandria, Va., that day and had come back and told Lincoln a story which pleased him so much that he broke out in a hearty laugh and said: 'I must tell you Tom Corwin's latest. Tom met an old man at Alexandria who knew George Washington, and he told Tom that George Washington often swore. Now, Corwin's father had always held the father of our country up as a faultless person and told his son to follow in his footsteps.

""""Well," said Corwin, "when I heard that George Washington was addicted to the vices and infirmities of man, I felt so relieved that I just shouted for joy.""""

"CATCH 'EM AND CHEAT 'EM"

The lawyers on the circuit traveled by Lincoln got together one night and tried him on the charge of accepting fees which tended to lower the established rates. It was the understood rule that a lawyer should accept all the client could be induced to pay. The tribunal was known as "The Ogmathorial Court."

Ward Lamon, his law partner at the time, tells about it:

"Lincoln was found guilty and fined for his awful crime against the pockets of his brethren of the bar. The fine he paid with great good humor, and then kept the crowd of lawyers in uproarious laughter until after midnight.

"He persisted in his revolt, however, declaring that with his consent his firm should never during its life, or after its dissolution, deserve the reputation enjoyed by those shining lights of the profession, 'Catch 'em and Cheat 'em.'"

A JURYMAN'S SCORN

Lincoln had assisted in the prosecution of a man who had robbed his neighbor's hen roosts. Jogging home along the highway with the foreman of the jury that had convicted the hen stealer, he was complimented by Lincoln on the zeal and ability of the prosecution, and remarked: "Why, when the country was young, and I was stronger than I am now, I didn't mind packing off a sheep now and again, but stealing hens!" The good man's scorn could not find words to express his opinion of a man who would steal hens.

HE "BROKE" TO WIN

A lawyer, who was a stranger to Mr. Lincoln, once expressed to General Linder the opinion that Mr. Lincoln's practice of telling stories to the jury was a waste of time.

"Don't lay that flattering unction to your soul," Linder answered; "Lincoln is like Tansey's horse, he 'breaks to win.'"

HAD RESPECT FOR THE EGGS

Early in 1831, "Abe" was one of the guests of honor at a boat-launching, he and two others having built the craft. The affair was a notable one, people being present from the territory surrounding. A large party came from Springfield with an ample supply of whisky, to give the boat and its builders a send-off. It was a sort of bipartisan mass-meeting, but there was one prevailing spirit, that born of rye and corn. Speeches were made in the best of feeling, some in favor of Andrew Jackson and some in favor of Henry Clay. Abraham Lincoln, the cook, told a number of funny stories, and it is recorded that they were not of too refined a character to suit the taste of his audience. A sleight-of-hand performer was present, and among other tricks performed, he fried some eggs in Lincoln's hat. Judge Herndon says, as explanatory to the delay in passing up the hat for the experiment, Lincoln drolly observed: "It was out of respect for the eggs, not care for my hat."

PRAISES HIS RIVAL FOR OFFICE.

When Mr. Lincoln was a candidate for the Legislature, it was the practice at that date in Illinois for two rival candidates to travel over the district together. The custom led to much good-natured raillery between them; and in such contests Lincoln was rarely, if ever, worsted. He could even turn the generosity of a rival to account by his whimsical treatment.

On one occasion, says Mr. Weir, a former resident of Sangamon county, he had driven out from Springfield in company with a political opponent to engage in joint debate. The carriage, it seems, belonged to his opponent. In addressing the gathering of farmers that met them, Lincoln was lavish in praise of the generosity of his friend.

"I am too poor to own a carriage," he said, "but my friend has generously invited me to ride with him. I want you to vote for me if you will; but if not then vote for my opponent, for he is a fine man."

His extravagant and persistent praise of his opponent appealed to the sense of humor in his rural audience, to whom his inability to own a carriage was by no means a disqualification.

NIAGARA FALLS

(Written By Abraham Lincoln)

The following article on Niagara Falls, in Mr. Lincoln's handwriting, was found among his papers after his death:

"Niagara Falls! By what mysterious power is it that millions and millions are drawn from all parts of the world to gaze upon Niagara Falls? There is no mystery about the thing itself. Every effect is just as any intelligent man, knowing the causes, would anticipate without seeing it. If the water moving onward in a great river reaches a point where there is a perpendicular jog of a hundred feet in descent in the bottom of the river, it is plain the water will have a violent and continuous plunge at that point. It is also plain, the water, thus plunging, will foam and roar, and send up a mist continuously, in which last, during sunshine, there will be perpetual rainbows. The mere physical of Niagara Falls is only this. Yet this is really a very small part of that world's wonder. Its power to excite reflection and emotion is its great charm. The geologist will demonstrate that the plunge, or fall, was once at Lake Ontario, and has worn its way back to its present position; he will ascertain how fast it is wearing now, and so get a basis for determining how long it has been wearing back from Lake Ontario, and finally demonstrate by it that this world is at least fourteen thousand years old. A philosopher of a slightly different turn will say, 'Niagara Falls is only the lip of the basin out of which pours all the surplus water which rains down on two or three hundred thousand square miles of the earth's surface.' He will estimate with approximate accuracy that five hundred thousand tons of water fall with their full weight a distance of a hundred feet each minute--thus exerting a force equal to the lifting of the same weight, through the same space, in the same time.

"But still there is more. It calls up the indefinite past. When Columbus first sought this continent--when Christ suffered on the cross--when Moses led Israel through the Red Sea--nay, even when Adam first came from the hand of his Maker; then, as now, Niagara was roaring here. The eyes of that species of extinct giants whose bones fill the mounds of America have gazed on Niagara, as ours do now. Contemporary with the first race of men, and older than the first man, Niagara is strong and fresh to-day as ten thousand years ago. The

Mammoth and Mastodon, so long dead that fragments of their monstrous bones alone testify that they ever lived, have gazed on Niagara--in that long, long time never still for a single moment (never dried), never froze, never slept, never rested."

MADE IT HOT FOR LINCOLN

A lady relative, who lived for two years with the Lincolns, said that Mr. Lincoln was in the habit of lying on the floor with the back of a chair for a pillow when he read.

One evening, when in this position in the hall, a knock was heard at the front door, and, although in his shirtsleeves, he answered the call. Two ladies were at the door, whom he invited into the parlor, notifying them in his open, familiar way, that he would "trot the women folks out."

Mrs. Lincoln, from an adjoining room, witnessed the ladies' entrance, and, overhearing her husband's jocose expression, her indignation was so instantaneous she made the situation exceedingly interesting for him, and he was glad to retreat from the house. He did not return till very late at night, and then slipped quietly in at a rear door.

WOULDN'T HOLD TITLE AGAINST HIM

During the rebellion the Austrian Minister to the United States Government introduced to the President a count, a subject of the Austrian government, who was desirous of obtaining a position in the American army.

Being introduced by the accredited Minister of Austria he required no further recommendation to secure the appointment; but, fearing that his importance might not be fully appreciated by the republican President, the count was particular in impressing the fact upon him that he bore that title, and that his family was ancient and highly respectable.

President Lincoln listened with attention, until this unnecessary commendation was mentioned; then, with a merry twinkle in his eye, he tapped the aristocratic sprig of hereditary nobility on the shoulder in the most fatherly way, as if the gentleman had made a confession of some unfortunate circumstance connected with his lineage, for which he was in no way responsible, and said:

"Never mind, you shall be treated with just as much consideration for all that. I will see to it that your bearing a title shan't hurt you."

ONLY ONE LIFE TO LIVE

A young man living in Kentucky had been enticed into the rebel army. After a few months he became disgusted, and managed to make his way back home. Soon after his arrival, the Union officer in command of the military stationed in the town had him arrested as a rebel spy, and, after a military trial he was condemned to be hanged.

President Lincoln was seen by one of his friends from Kentucky, who explained his errand and asked for mercy. "Oh, yes, I understand; some one has been crying, and worked upon your feelings, and you have come here to work on mine."

His friend then went more into detail, and assured him of his belief in the truth of the story. After some deliberation, Mr. Lincoln, evidently scarcely more than half convinced, but still preferring to err on the side of mercy, replied:

"If a man had more than one life, I think a little hanging would not hurt this one; but after he is once dead we cannot bring him back, no matter how sorry we may be; so the boy shall be pardoned."

And a reprieve was given on the spot.

WHEN MONEY MIGHT BE USED

Some Lincoln enthusiast in Kansas, with much more pretensions than power, wrote him in March, 1860 proposing to furnish a Lincoln delegation from that State to the Chicago Convention, and suggesting that Lincoln should pay the legitimate expenses of organizing, electing, and taking to the convention the promised Lincoln delegates.

To this Lincoln replied that "in the main, the use of money is wrong, but for certain objects in a political contest the use of some is both right and indispensable." And he added: "If you shall be appointed a delegate to Chicago, I will furnish $100 to bear the expenses of the trip."

He heard nothing further from the Kansas man until he saw an announcement in the newspapers that Kansas had elected delegates and instructed them for Seward.

BIG ENOUGH HOG FOR HIM

To a curiosity-seeker who desired a permit to pass the lines to visit the field of Bull Run, after the first battle, Lincoln made the following reply:

"A man in Cortlandt county raised a porker of such unusual size that strangers went out of their way to see it.

"One of them the other day met the old gentleman and inquired about the animal.

"'Wall, yes,' the old fellow said, 'I've got such a critter, mi'ty big un; but I guess I'll have to charge you about a shillin' for lookin' at him.'

"The stranger looked at the old man for a minute or so, pulled out the desired coin, handed it to him and started to go off. 'Hold on,' said the other. 'don't you want to see the hog?'

"'No,' said the stranger; 'I have seen as big a hog as I want to see!'

"And you will find that fact the case with yourself, if you should happen to see a few live rebels there as well as dead ones."

CREDITOR PAID DEBTORS DEBT

A certain rich man in Springfield, Illinois, sued a poor attorney for $2.50, and Lincoln was asked to prosecute the case. Lincoln urged the creditor to let the matter drop, adding, "You can make nothing out of him, and it will cost you a good deal more than the debt to bring suit." The creditor was still determined to have his way, and threatened to seek some other attorney. Lincoln then said, "Well, if you are determined that suit should be brought, I will bring it; but my charge will be $10."

The money was paid him, and peremptory orders were given that the suit be brought that day. After the client's departure Lincoln went out of the office, returning in about an hour with an amused look on his face.

Asked what pleased him, he replied, "I brought suit against --, and then hunted him up, told him what I had done, handed him half of the $10, and we went over to the squire's office. He confessed judgment and paid the bill."

Lincoln added that he didn't see any other way to make things satisfactory for his client as well as the other.

EVERY FELLOW FOR HIMSELF

An elegantly dressed young Virginian assured Lincoln that he had done a great deal of hard manual labor in his time. Much amused at this solemn declaration, Lincoln said:

"Oh, yes; you Virginians shed barrels of perspiration while standing off at a distance and superintending the work your slaves do for you. It is different with us. Here it is every fellow for himself, or he doesn't get there."

NO "SECOND COMING" FOR SPRINGFIELD

Soon after the opening of Congress in 1861, Mr. Shannon, from California, made the customary call at the White House. In the conversation that ensued, Mr Shannon said: "Mr. President, I met an old friend of yours in California last summer, a Mr. Campbell, who had a good deal to say of your Springfield life."

"Ah!" returned Mr. Lincoln, "I am glad to hear of him. Campbell used to be a dry fellow in those days," he continued. "For a time he was Secretary of State. One day during the legislative vacation, a meek, cadaverous-looking man, with a white neckcloth, introduced himself to him at his office, and, stating that he had been informed that Mr. C. had the letting of the hall of representatives, he wished to secure it, if possible, for a course of lectures he desired to deliver in Springfield.

"'May I ask,' said the Secretary, 'what is to be the subject of your lectures?'

"'Certainly,' was the reply, with a very solemn expression of countenance. 'The course I wish to deliver is on the Second Coming of our Lord.'

"'It is of no use,' said C.; 'if you will take my advice, you will not waste your time in this city. It is my private opinion that, if the Lord has been in Springfield once, He will never come the second time!'"

DON'T AIM TOO HIGH

"Billy, don't shoot too high--aim lower, and the common people will understand you," Lincoln once said to a brother lawyer.

"They are the ones you want to reach--at least, they are the ones you ought to reach.

"The educated and refined people will understand you, anyway. If you aim too high, your idea will go over the heads of the masses, and only hit those who need no hitting."

NOT MUCH AT RAIL-SPLITTING

One who afterward became one of Lincoln's most devoted friends and adherents tells this story regarding the manner in which Lincoln received him when they met for the first time:

"After a comical survey of my fashionable toggery,--my swallow-tail coat, white neck-cloth, and ruffled shirt (an astonishing outfit for a young limb of the law in that settlement), Lincoln said:

"'Going to try your hand at the law, are you? I should know at a glance that you were a Virginian; but I don't think you would succeed at splitting rails. That was my occupation at your age, and I don't think I have taken as much pleasure in anything else from that day to this.'"

SURE CURE FOR BOILS

President Lincoln and Postmaster-General Blair were talking of the war.

"Blair," said the President, "did you ever know that fright has sometimes proven a cure for boils?" "No, Mr. President, how is that?" "I'll tell you. Not long ago when a colonel, with his cavalry, was at the front, and the Rebs were making things rather lively for us, the colonel was ordered out to a reconnoissance. He was troubled at the time with a big boil where it made horseback riding decidedly uncomfortable. He finally dismounted and ordered the troops forward without him. Soon he was startled by the rapid reports of pistols and the helter-skelter approach of his troops in full retreat before a yelling rebel force. He forgot everything but the yells, sprang into his saddle, and made capital time over the fences and ditches till safe within the lines. The pain from his boil was gone, and the boil, too, and the colonel swore that there was no cure for boils so sure as fright from rebel yells."

FAVORED THE OTHER SIDE

Lincoln was candor itself when conducting his side of a case in court. General Mason Brayman tells this story as an illustration:

"It is well understood by the profession that lawyers do not read authores favoring the opposite side. I once heard Mr. Lincoln, in the Supreme Court of Illinois, reading from a reported case some strong points in favor of his argument. Reading a little too far, and before becoming aware of it, plunged into an authority against himself.

"Pausing a moment, he drew up his shoulders in a comical way, and half laughing, went on, 'There, there, may it please the court, I reckon I've scratched up a snake. But, as I'm in for it, I guess I'll read it through.'

"Then, in his most ingenious and matchless manner, he went on with his argument, and won his case, convincing the court that it was not much of a snake after all."

"FIND OUT FOR YOURSELVES"

"Several of us lawyers," remarked one of his colleagues, "in the eastern end of the circuit, annoyed Lincoln once while he was holding court for Davis by attempting to defend against a note to which there were many makers. We had no legal, but a good moral defense, but what we wanted most of all was to stave it off till the next term of court by one expedient or another.

"We bothered 'the court' about it till late on Saturday, the day of adjournment. He adjourned for supper with nothing left but this case to dispose of. After supper he heard our twaddle for nearly an hour, and then made this odd entry.

"'L. D. Chaddon vs. J. D. Beasley et al. April Term, 1856. Champaign county Court. Plea in abatement by B. Z. Green, a defendant not served, filed Saturday at 11 o'clock a. m., April 24, 1856, stricken from the files by order of court. Demurrer to declaration, if there ever was one, overruled. Defendants who are served now, at 8 o'clock p. m., of the last day of the term, ask to plead to the merits, which is denied by the court on the ground that the offer comes too late, and therefore, as by nil dicet, judgment is rendered for Pl'ff. Clerk assess damages. A. Lincoln, Judge pro tem.'

"The lawyer who reads this singular entry will appreciate its oddity if no one else does. After making it, one of the lawyers, on recovering from his astonishment, ventured to enquire: 'Well, Lincoln, how can we get this case up again?'

"Lincoln eyed him quizzically for a moment, and then answered, 'You have all been so mighty smart about this case, you can find out how to take it up again yourselves.'"

ROUGH ON THE NEGRO

Mr. Lincoln, one day, was talking with the Rev. Dr. Sunderland about the Emancipation Proclamation and the future of the negro. Suddenly a ripple of amusement broke the solemn tone of his voice. "As for the negroes, Doctor, and what is going to become of them: I told Ben Wade the other day, that it made me think of a story I read in one of my first books, 'Aesop's Fables.' It was an old edition, and had curious rough wood cuts, one of which showed three white men scrubbing a negro in a potash kettle filled with cold water. The text explained that the men thought that by scrubbing the negro they might make him white. Just about the time they thought they were succeeding, he took cold and died. Now, I am afraid that by the time we get through this War the negro will catch cold and die."

GRANT'S BRAND OF WHISKEY

Lincoln was not a man of impulse, and did nothing upon the spur of the moment; action with him was the result of deliberation and study. He took nothing for granted; he judged men by their performances and not their speech.

If a general lost battles, Lincoln lost confidence in him; if a commander was successful, Lincoln put him where he would be of the most service to the country.

"Grant is a drunkard," asserted powerful and influential politicians to the President at the White House time after time; "he is not himself half the time; he can't be relied upon, and it is a shame to have such a man in command of an army."

"So Grant gets drunk, does he?" queried Lincoln, addressing himself to one of the particularly active detractors of the soldier, who, at that period, was inflicting heavy damage upon the Confederates.

"Yes, he does, and I can prove it," was the reply.

"Well," returned Lincoln, with the faintest suspicion of a twinkle in his eye, "you needn't waste your time getting proof; you just find out, to oblige me, what brand of whiskey Grant drinks, because I want to send a barrel of it to each one of my generals."

That ended the crusade against Grant, so far as the question of drinking was concerned.

"SOME UGLY OLD LAWYER"

A. W. Swan, of Albuquerque, New Mexico, told this story on Lincoln, being an eyewitness of the scene:

"One day President Lincoln was met in the park between the White House and the War Department by an irate private soldier, who was swearing in a high key, cursing the Government from the President down. Mr. Lincoln paused and asked him what was the matter. 'Matter enough,' was the reply. 'I want my money. I have been discharged here, and can't get my pay.' Mr. Lincoln asked if he had his papers, saying that he used to practice law in a small way, and possibly could help him.

"My friend and I stepped behind some convenient shrubbery where we could watch the result. Mr. Lincoln took the papers from the hands of the crippled soldier, and sat down with him at the foot of a convenient tree, where he examined them carefully, and writing a line on the back, told the soldier to take them to Mr. Potts, Chief Clerk of the War Department, who would doubtless attend to the matter at once.

"After Mr. Lincoln had left the soldier, we stepped out and asked him if he knew whom he had been talking with. 'Some ugly old fellow who pretends to be a lawyer,' was the reply. My companion asked to see the papers, and on their being handed to him, pointed to the indorsement they had received: This indorsement read

"'Mr. Potts, attend to this man's case at once and see that he gets his pay. A. L.'"

GOOD MEMORY OF NAMES

The following story illustrates the power of Mr. Lincoln's memory of names and faces. When he was a comparatively young man, and a candidate for the Illinois Legislature, he made a personal canvass of the district. While "swinging around the circle" he stopped one day and took dinner with a farmer in Sangamon county.

Years afterward, when Mr. Lincoln had become President, a soldier came to call on him at the White House. At the first glance the Chief Executive said: "Yes, I remember; you used to live on the Danville road. I took dinner with you when I was running for the Legislature. I recollect that we stood talking out at the barnyard gate while I sharpened my jackknife."

"Y-a-a-s," drawled the soldier, "you did. But say, wherever did you put that whetstone? I looked for it a dozen times, but I never could find it after the day you used it. We allowed as how mabby you took it 'long with you."

"No," said Lincoln, looking serious and pushing away a lot of documents of state from the desk in front of him. "No, I put it on top of that gatepost--that high one."

"Well!" exclaimed the visitor, "mabby you did. Couldn't anybody else have put it there, and none of us ever thought of looking there for it."

The soldier was then on his way home, and when he got there the first thing he did was to look for the whetstone. And sure enough, there it was, just where Lincoln had laid it fifteen years before. The honest fellow wrote a letter to the Chief Magistrate, telling him that the whetstone had been found, and would never be lost again.

SETTLED OUT OF COURT

When Abe Lincoln used to be drifting around the country, practicing law in Fulton and Menard counties, Illinois, an old fellow met him going to Lewiston, riding a horse which, while it was a serviceable enough animal, was not of the kind to be truthfully called a fine saddler. It was a weatherbeaten nag, patient and plodding, and it toiled along with Abe--and Abe's books, tucked away in saddle-bags, lay heavy on the horse's flank.

"Hello, Uncle Tommy," said Abe.

"Hello, Abe," responded Uncle Tommy. "I'm powerful glad to see ye, Abe, fer I'm gwyne to have sumthin' fer ye at Lewiston co't, I reckon."

"How's that, Uncle Tommy?" said Abe.

"Well, Jim Adams, his land runs 'long o' mine, he's pesterin' me a heap an' I got to get the law on Jim, I reckon."

"Uncle Tommy, you haven't had any fights with Jim, have you?"

"No."

"He's a fair to middling neighbor, isn't he?"

"Only tollable, Abe."

"He's been a neighbor of yours for a long time, hasn't he?"

"Nigh on to fifteen year."

"Part of the time you get along all right, don't you?"

"I reckon we do, Abe."

"Well, now, Uncle Tommy, you see this horse of mine? He isn't as good a horse as I could straddle, and I sometimes get out of patience with him, but I know his faults. He does fairly well as horses go, and it might take me a long time to get used to some other horse's faults. For all horses have faults. You and Uncle Jimmy must put up with each other as I and my horse do with one another."

"I reckon, Abe," said Uncle Tommy, as he bit off about four ounces of Missouri plug. "I reckon you're about right."

And Abe Lincoln, with a smile on his gaunt face, rode on toward Lewiston.

SENTINEL OBEYED ORDERS.

A slight variation of the traditional sentry story is related by C. C. Buel. It was a cold, blusterous winter night. Says Mr. Buel:

"Mr. Lincoln emerged from the front door, his lank figure bent over as he drew tightly about his shoulders the shawl which he employed for such protection; for he was on his way to the War Department, at the west corner of the grounds, where in times of battle he was wont to get the midnight dispatches from the field. As the blast struck him he thought of the numbness of the pacing sentry, and, turning to him, said: 'Young man, you've got a cold job to-night; step inside, and stand guard there.'

"'My orders keep me out here,' the soldier replied.

"'Yes,' said the President, in his argumentative tone; 'but your duty can be performed just as well inside as out here, and you'll oblige me by going in.'

"'I have been stationed outside,' the soldier answered, and resumed his beat.

"'Hold on there!' said Mr. Lincoln, as he turned back again; 'it occurs to me that I am Commander-in-Chief of the army, and I order you to go inside.'"

WHY LINCOLN GROWED WHISKERS

Perhaps the majority of people in the United States don't know why Lincoln "growed" whiskers after his first nomination for the Presidency. Before that time his face was clean shaven.

In the beautiful village of Westfield, Chautauqua county, New York, there lived, in 1860, little Grace Bedell. During the campaign of that year she saw a portrait of Lincoln, for whom she felt the love and reverence that was common in Republican families, and his smooth, homely face rather disappointed her. She said to her mother: "I think, mother, that Mr. Lincoln would look better if he wore whiskers, and I mean to write and tell him so."

The mother gave her permission.

Grace's father was a Republican; her two brothers were Democrats. Grace wrote at once to the "Hon. Abraham Lincoln, Esq., Springfield, Illinois," in which she told him how old she was, and where she lived; that she was a Republican; that she thought he would make a good President, but would look better if he would let his whiskers grow. If he would do so, she would try to coax her brothers to vote for him. She thought the rail fence around the picture of his cabin was very pretty. "If you have not time to answer my letter, will you allow your little girl to reply for you?"

Lincoln was much pleased with the letter, and decided to answer it, which he did at once, as follows:

"Springfield, Illinois, October i9, 1860.

"Miss Grace Bedell.

"My Dear Little Miss: Your very agreeable letter of the fifteenth is received. I regret the necessity of saying I have no daughter. I have three sons; one seventeen, one nine and one seven years of age. They, with their mother, constitute my whole family. As to the whiskers, having never worn any, do you not think people would call it a piece of silly affectation if I should begin it now? Your very sincere well-wisher, A. LINCOLN."

When on the journey to Washington to be inaugurated, Lincoln's train stopped at Westfield. He recollected his little correspondent and spoke of her to ex-Lieutenant Governor George W. Patterson, who called out and asked if Grace Bedell was present.

There was a large surging mass of people gathered about the train, but Grace was discovered at a distance; the crowd opened a pathway to the coach, and she came, timidly but gladly, to the President-elect, who told her that she might see that he had allowed his whiskers to grow at her request. Then, reaching out his long arms, he drew her up to him and kissed her. The act drew an enthusiastic demonstration of approval from the multitude.

Grace married a Kansas banker, and became Grace Bedell Billings.

LINCOLN AS A DANCER

Lincoln made his first appearance in society when he was first sent to Springfield, Ill., as a member of the State Legislature. It was not an imposing figure which he cut in a ballroom, but still he was occasionally to be found there. Miss Mary Todd, who afterward became his wife, was the magnet which drew the tall, awkward young man from his den. One evening Lincoln approached Miss Todd, and said, in his peculiar idiom:

"Miss Todd, I should like to dance with you the worst way." The young woman accepted the inevitable, and hobbled around the room with him. When she returned to her seat, one of her companions asked mischievously

"Well, Mary, did he dance with you the worst way."

"Yes," she answered, "the very worst."

SIMPLY PRACTICAL HUMANITY

An instance of young Lincoln's practical humanity at an early period of his life is recorded in this way:

One evening, while returning from a "raising" in his wide neighborhood, with a number of companions, he discovered a stray horse, with saddle and bridle upon him. The horse was recognized as belonging to a man who was accustomed to get drunk, and it was suspected at once that he was not far off. A short search only was necessary to confirm the belief.

The poor drunkard was found in a perfectly helpless condition, upon the chilly ground. Abraham's companions urged the cowardly policy of leaving him to his fate, but young Lincoln would not hear to the proposition.

At his request, the miserable sot was lifted on his shoulders, and he actually carried him eighty rods to the nearest house.

Sending word to his father that he should not be back that night, with the reason for his absence, he attended and nursed the man until the morning, and had the pleasure of believing that he had saved his life.

HAPPY FIGURES OF SPEECH

On one occasion, exasperated at the discrepancy between the aggregate of troops forwarded to McClellan and the number that same general reported as having received, Lincoln exclaimed: "Sending men to that army is like shoveling fleas across a barnyard--half of them never get there."

To a politician who had criticised his course, he wrote: "Would you have me drop the War where it is, or would you prosecute it in future with elder stalk squirts charged with rosewater?"

When, on his first arrival in Washington as President, he found himself besieged by office-seekers, while the War was breaking out, he said: "I feel like a man letting lodgings at one end of his house while the other end is on fire."

JUST LIKE SEWARD

The first corps of the army commanded by General Reynolds was once reviewed by the President on a beautiful plain at the north of Potomac Creek, about eight miles from Hooker's headquarters. The party rode thither in an ambulance over a rough corduroy road, and as they passed over some of the more difficult portions of the jolting way the ambulance driver, who sat well in front, occasionally let fly a volley of suppressed oaths at his wild team of six mules.

Finally, Mr. Lincoln, leaning forward, touched the man on the shoulder and said

"Excuse me, my friend, are you an Episcopalian?"

The man, greatly startled, looked around and replied:

"No, Mr. President; I am a Methodist."

"Well," said Lincoln, "I thought you must be an Episcopalian, because you swear just like Governor Seward, who is a church warder."

THOUGHT GOD WOULD HAVE TOLD HIM

Professor Jonathan Baldwin Turner was one of the few men to whom Mr. Lincoln confided his intention to issue the Proclamation of Emancipation.

Mr. Lincoln told his Illinois friend of the visit of a delegation to him who claimed to have a message from God that the War would not be successful without the freeing of the negroes, to whom Mr. Lincoln replied: "Is it not a little strange that He should tell this to you, who have so little to do with it, and should not have told me, who has a great deal to do with it?"

At the same time he informed Professor Turner he had his Proclamation in his pocket.

TOOK NOTHING BUT MONEY

During the War Congress appropriated $10,000 to be expended by the President in defending United States Marshals in cases of arrests and seizures where the legality of their actions was tested in the courts. Previously the Marshals sought the assistance of the Attorney-General in defending them, but when they found that the President had a fund for that purpose they sought to control the money.

In speaking of these Marshals one day, Mr. Lincoln said:

"They are like a man in Illinois, whose cabin was burned down, and, according to the kindly custom of early days in the West, his neighbors all contributed something to start him again. In his case they had been so liberal that he soon found himself better off than before the fire, and he got proud. One day a neighbor brought him a bag of oats, but the fellow refused it with scorn.

"'No,' said he, 'I'm not taking oats now. I take nothing but money.'"

WOULD BLOW THEM TO H---

Mr. Lincoln had advised Lieutenant-General Winfield Scott, commanding the United States Army, of the threats of violence on inauguration day, 1861. General Scott was sick in bed at Washington when Adjutant-General Thomas Mather, of Illinois, called upon him in President-elect Lincoln's behalf, and the veteran commander was much wrought up. Said he to General Mather:

"Present my compliments to Mr. Lincoln when you return to Springfield, and tell him I expect him to come on to Washington as soon as he is ready; say to him that I will look after those Maryland and Virginia rangers myself. I will plant cannon at both ends of Pennsylvania avenue, and if any of them show their heads or raise a finger, I'll blow them to h---."

"YANKEE" GOODNESS OF HEART

One day, when the President was with the troops who were fighting at the front, the wounded, both Union and Confederate, began to pour in.

As one stretcher was passing Lincoln, he heard the voice of a lad calling to his mother in agonizing tones. His great heart filled. He forgot the crisis of the hour. Stopping the carriers, he knelt, and bending over him, asked: "What can I do for you, my poor child?"

"Oh, you will do nothing for me," he replied. "You are a Yankee. I cannot hope that my message to my mother will ever reach her."

Lincoln, in tears, his voice full of tenderest love, convinced the boy of his sincerity, and he gave his good-bye words without reserve.

The President directed them copied, and ordered that they be sent that night, with a flag of truce, into the enemy's lines.

WALKED AS HE TALKED

When Mr. Lincoln made his famous humorous speech in Congress ridiculing General Cass, he began to speak from notes, but, as he warmed up, he left his desk and his notes, to stride down the alley toward the Speaker's chair.

Occasionally, as he would complete a sentence amid shouts of laughter, he would return up the alley to his desk, consult his notes, take a sip of water and start off again.

Mr. Lincoln received many congratulations at the close, Democrats joining the Whigs in their complimentary comments.

One Democrat, however (who had been nicknamed "Sausage" Sawyer), didn't enthuse at all.

"Sawyer," asked an Eastern Representative, "how did you like the lanky Illinoisan's speech? Very able, wasn't it?"

"Well," replied Sawyer, "the speech was pretty good, but I hope he won't charge mileage on his travels while delivering it."

THE SONG DID THE BUSINESS.

The Virginia (Ill.) Enquirer, of March 1, 1879, tells this story:

"John McNamer was buried last Sunday, near Petersburg, Menard county. A long while ago he was Assessor and Treasurer of the County for several successive terms. Mr. McNamer was an early settler in that section, and, before the town of Petersburg was laid out, in business in Old Salem, a village that existed many years ago two miles south of the present site of Petersburg.

"'Abe' Lincoln was then postmaster of the place and sold whisky to its inhabitants. There are old-timers yet living in Menard who bought many a jug of corn-juice from 'Old Abe' when he lived at Salem. It was here that Anne Rutledge dwelt, and in whose grave Lincoln wrote that his heart was buried.

"As the story runs, the fair and gentle Anne was originally John McNamer's sweetheart, but 'Abe' took a 'shine' to the young lady, and succeeded in heading off McNamer and won her affections. But Anne Rutledge died, and Lincoln went to Springfield, where he some time afterwards married.

"It is related that during the War a lady belonging to a prominent Kentucky family visited Washington to beg for her son's pardon, who was then in prison under sentence of death for belonging to a band of guerrillas who had committed many murders and outrages.

"With the mother was her daughter, a beautiful young lady, who was an accomplished musician. Mr. Lincoln received the visitors in his usual kind manner, and the mother made known the object of her visit, accompanying her plea with tears and sobs and all the customary romantic incidents.

"There were probably extenuating circumstances in favor of the young rebel prisoner, and while the President seemed to be deeply pondering the young lady moved to a piano near by and taking a seat commenced to sing 'Gentle Annie,' a very sweet and pathetic ballad which, before the War, was a familiar song in almost every household in the Union, and is not yet entirely forgotten, for that matter.

"It is to be presumed that the young lady sang the song with more plaintiveness and effect than 'Old Abe' had ever heard it in Springfield. During its rendition, he arose from his seat, crossed the room to a window in the westward, through which he gazed for several minutes with a 'sad, far-away look,' which has so often been noted as one of his peculiarities.

"His memory, no doubt, went back to the days of his humble life on the Sangamon, and with visions of Old Salem and its rustic people, who once gathered in his primitive store, came a picture of the 'Gentle Annie' of his youth, whose ashes had rested for many long years under the wild flowers and brambles of the old rural burying-ground, but whose spirit then, perhaps, guided him to the side of mercy.

"Be that as it may, President Lincoln drew a large red silk handkerchief from his coatpocket, with which he wiped his face vigorously. Then he turned, advanced quickly to his desk, wrote a brief note, which he handed to the lady, and informed her that it was the pardon she sought.

"The scene was no doubt touching in a great degree and proves that a nice song, well sung, has often a powerful influence in recalling tender recollections. It proves, also, that Abraham Lincoln was a man of fine feelings, and that, if the occurrence was a put-up job on the lady's part, it accomplished the purpose all the same."

A "FREE FOR ALL"

Lincoln made a political speech at Pappsville, Illinois, when a candidate for the Legislature the first time. A free-for-all fight began soon after the opening of the meeting, and Lincoln, noticing one of his friends about to succumb to the energetic attack of an infuriated ruffian, edged his way through the crowd, and, seizing the bully by the neck and the seat of his trousers, threw him, by means of his strength and long arms, as one witness stoutly insists, "twelve feet away." Returning to the stand, and throwing aside his hat, he inaugurated his campaign with the following brief but pertinent declaration

"Fellow-citizens, I presume you all know who I am. I am humble Abraham Lincoln. I have been solicited by many friends to become a candidate for the Legislature. My politics are short and sweet, like the old woman's dance. I am in favor of the national bank; I am in favor of the internal improvement system and a high protective tariff. These are my sentiments; if elected, I shall be thankful; if not, it will be all the same."

THREE INFERNAL BORES

One day, when President Lincoln was alone and busily engaged on an important subject, involving vexation and anxiety, he was disturbed by the unwarranted intrusion of three men, who, without apology, proceeded to lay their claim before him.

The spokesman of the three reminded the President that they were the owners of some torpedo or other warlike invention which, if the government would only adopt it, would soon crush the rebellion.

"Now," said the spokesman, "we have been here to see you time and again; you have referred us to the Secretary of War, the Chief of Ordnance, and the General of the Army, and they give us no satisfaction. We have been kept here waiting, till money and patience are exhausted, and we now come to demand of you a final reply to our application."

Mr. Lincoln listened to this insolent tirade, and at its close the old twinkle came into his eye.

"You three gentlemen remind me of a story I once heard," said he, "of a poor little boy out West who had lost his mother. His father wanted to give him a religious education, and so placed him in the family of a clergyman, whom he directed to instruct the little fellow carefully in the Scriptures. Every day the boy had to commit to memory and recite one chapter of the Bible. Things proceeded smoothly until they reached that chapter which details the story of the trial of Shadrach, Meshach and Abednego in the fiery furnace. When asked to repeat these three names the boy said he had forgotten them.

"His teacher told him that he must learn them, and gave him another day to do so. The next day the boy again forgot them.

"'Now,' said the teacher, 'you have again failed to remember those names and you can go no farther until you have learned them. I will give you another day on this lesson, and if you don't repeat the names I will punish you.'

"A third time the boy came to recite, and got down to the stumbling block, when the clergyman said: 'Now tell me the names of the men in the fiery furnace.'

"'Oh,' said the boy, 'here come those three infernal bores! I wish the devil had them!'"

Having received their "final answer," the three patriots retired, and at the Cabinet meeting which followed, the President, in high good humor, related how he had dismissed his unwelcome visitors.

A SLOW HORSE

On one occasion when Mr. Lincoln was going to attend a political convention one of his rivals, a liveryman, provided him with a slow horse, hoping that he would not reach his destination in time. Mr. Lincoln got there, however, and when he returned with the horse he said: "You keep this horse for funerals, don't you?" "Oh, no," replied the liveryman. "Well, I'm glad of that, for if you did you'd never get a corpse to the grave in time for the resurrection."

A GREENBACK LEGEND

At a Cabinet meeting once, the advisability of putting a legend on greenbacks similar to the In God We Trust legend on the silver coins was discussed, and the President was asked what his view was. He replied: "If you are going to put a legend on the greenback, I would suggest that of Peter and Paul: 'Silver and gold we have not, but what we have we'll give you.'"

MATRIMONIAL ADVICE

For a while during the Civil War, General Fremont was without a command. One day in discussing Fremont's case with George W. Julian, President Lincoln said he did not know where to place him, and that it reminds him of the old man who advised his son to take a wife, to which the young man responded: "All right; whose wife shall I take?"

OWED LOTS OF MONEY

On April 14, 1865, a few hours previous to his assassination, President Lincoln sent a message by Congressman Schuyler Colfax, Vice-President during General Grant's first term, to the miners in the Rocky Mountains and the regions bounded by the Pacific ocean, in which he said:

"Now that the Rebellion is overthrown, and we know pretty nearly the amount of our National debt, the more gold and silver we mine, we make the payment of that debt so much easier.

"Now I am going to encourage that in every possible way. We shall have hundreds of thousands of disbanded soldiers, and many have feared that their return home in such great numbers might paralyze industry by furnishing, suddenly, a greater supply of labor than there will be demand for. I am going to try to attract them to the hidden wealth of our mountain ranges, where there is room enough for all. Immigration, which even the War has not stopped, will land upon our shores hundreds of thousands more per year from overcrowded Europe. I intend to point them to the gold and silver that wait for them in the West.

"Tell the miners for me that I shall promote their interests to the utmost of my ability; because their prosperity as the prosperity of the nation; and," said he, his eye kindling with enthusiasm, "we shall prove, in a very few years, that we are indeed the treasury of the world."

"ON THE LORD'S SIDE"

President Lincoln made a significant remark to a clergyman in the early days of the War.

"Let us have faith, Mr. President," said the minister, "that the Lord is on our side in this great struggle."

Mr. Lincoln quietly answered: "I am not at all concerned about that, for I know that the Lord is always on the side of the right; but it is my constant anxiety and prayer that I and this nation may be on the Lord's side."

WANTED TO BE NEAR "ABE"

It was Lincoln's custom to hold an informal reception once a week, each caller taking his turn.

Upon one of these eventful days an old friend from Illinois stood in line for almost an hour. At last he was so near the President his voice could reach him, and, calling out to his old associate, he startled every one by exclaiming, "Hallo, 'Abe'; how are ye? I'm in line and hev come for an orfice, too."

Lincoln singled out the man with the stentorian voice, and recognizing

"a particularly old friend, one whose wife had befriended him at a peculiarly trying time, the President responded to his greeting in a cordial manner, and told him "to hang onto himself and not kick the traces. Keep in line and you'll soon get here."

They met and shook hands with the old fervor and renewed their friendship.

The informal reception over, Lincoln sent for his old friend, and the latter began to urge his claims.

After having given him some good advice, Lincoln kindly told him he was incapable of holding any such position as he asked for. The disappointment of the Illinois friend was plainly shown, and with a perceptible tremor in his voice he said, "Martha's dead, the gal is married, and I've guv Jim the forty."

Then looking at Lincoln he came a little nearer and almost whispered, "I knowed I wasn't eddicated enough to git the place, but I kinder want to stay where I ken see 'Abe' Lincoln."

He was given employment in the White House grounds.

Afterwards the President said, "These brief interviews, stripped of even the semblance of ceremony, give me a better insight into the real character of the person and his true reason for seeking one."

GOT HIS FOOT IN IT

William H. Seward, idol of the Republicans of the East, six months after Lincoln had made his "Divided House" speech, delivered an address at Rochester, New York, containing this famous sentence:

"It is an irrepressible conflict between opposing and enduring forces, and it means that the United States must, and will, sooner or later, become either entirely a slave-holding nation, or entirely a free-labor nation."

Seward, who had simply followed in Lincoln's steps, was defeated for the Presidential nomination at the Republican National Convention of 1860, because he was "too radical," and Lincoln, who was still "radicaler," was named.

SAVED BY A LETTER

The chief interest of the Illinois campaign of 1843 lay in the race for Congress in the Capital district, which was between Hardin--fiery, eloquent, and impetuous Democrat--and Lincoln-- plain, practical, and ennobled Whig. The world knows the result. Lincoln was elected.

It is not so much his election as the manner in which he secured his nomination with which we have to deal. Before that ever-memorable spring Lincoln vacillated between the courts of Springfield, rated as a plain, honest, logical Whig, with no ambition higher politically than to occupy some good home office.

Late in the fall of 1842 his name began to be mentioned in connection with Congressional aspirations, which fact greatly annoyed the leaders of his political party, who had already selected as the Whig candidate E. D. Baker, afterward the gallant Colonel who fell so bravely and died such an honorable death on the battlefield of Ball's Bluff.

Despite all efforts of his opponents within his party, the name of the "gaunt railsplitter" was hailed with acclaim by the masses, to whom he had endeared himself by his witticisms, honest tongue, and quaint philosophy when on the stump, or mingling with them in their homes.

The convention, which met in early spring, in the city of Springfield, was to be composed of the usual number of delegates. The contest for the nomination was spirited and exciting.

A few weeks before the meeting of the convention the fact was found by the leaders that the advantage lay with Lincoln, and that unless they pulled some very fine wires nothing could save Baker.

They attempted to play the game that has so often won, by "convincing" delegates under instructions for Lincoln to violate them, and vote for Baker. They had apparently succeeded.

"The best laid plans of mice and men gang aft agley." So it was in this case. Two days before the convention Lincoln received an intimation of this, and, late at night, wrote the following letter.

The letter was addressed to Martin Morris, who resided at Petersburg, an intimate friend of his, and by him circulated among those who were instructed for him at the county convention.

It had the desired effect. The convention met, the scheme of the conspirators miscarried, Lincoln was nominated, made a vigorous canvass, and was triumphantly elected, thus paving the way for his more extended and brilliant conquests.

This letter, Lincoln had often told his friends, gave him ultimately the Chief Magistracy of the nation. He has also said, that, had he been beaten before the convention, he would have been forever obscured. The following is a verbatim copy of the epistle

"April 14, 1843.

"Friend Morris: I have heard it intimated that Baker is trying to get you or Miles, or both of you, to violate the instructions of the meeting that appointed you, and to go for him. I have insisted, and still insist, that this cannot be true.

"Sure Baker would not do the like. As well might Hardin ask me to vote for him in the convention.

"Again, it is said there will be an attempt to get instructions in your county requiring you to go for Baker. This is all wrong. Upon the same rule, why might I not fly from the decision against me at Sangamon and get up instructions to their delegates to go for me. There are at least 1,200 Whigs in the county that took no part, and yet I would as soon stick my head in the fire as attempt it.

"Besides, if any one should get the nomination by such extraordinary means, all harmony in the district would inevitably be lost. Honest Whigs (and very nearly all of them are honest) would not quietly abide such enormities.

"I repeat, such an attempt on Baker's part cannot be true. Write me at Springfield how the matter is. Don't show or speak of this letter.

"A. LINCOLN."

Mr. Morris did show the letter, and Mr. Lincoln always thanked his stars that he did.

HIS FAVORITE POEM

Mr. Lincoln's favorite poem was "Oh! Why Should the Spirit of Mortal Be Proud?" written by William Knox, a Scotchman, although Mr. Lincoln never knew the author's name. He once said to a friend:

"This poem has been a great favorite with me for years. It was first shown to me, when a young man, by a friend. I afterward saw it and cut it from a newspaper and learned it by heart. I would give a great deal to know who wrote it, but I have never been able to ascertain."

"Oh! why should the spirit of mortal be proud?—
Like a swift-fleeing meteor, a fastflying cloud,
A flash of the lightning, a break of the wave,
He passeth from life to his rest in the grave.

"The leaves of the oak and the willow shall fade,
Be scattered around, and together be laid;
And the young and the old, and the low and the high,
Shall moulder to dust, and together shall lie.

"The infant a mother attended and loved;
The mother, that infant's affection who proved,
The husband, that mother and infant who blessed—
Each, all, are away to their dwellings of rest.

"The maid on whose cheek, on whose brow, in whose eye,
Shone beauty and pleasure--her triumphs are by;
And the memory of those who loved her and praised,
Are alike from the minds of the living erased.

"The hand of the king, that the sceptre hath borne,
The brow of the priest, that the mitre hath worn,
The eye of the sage, and the heart of the brave,
Are hidden and lost in the depths of the grave.

"The peasant, whose lot was to sow and to reap,
The herdsman, who climbed with his goats up the steep;
The beggar, who wandered in search of his bread,
Have faded away like the grass that we tread.

"The saint, who enjoyed the communion of heaven,
The sinner, who dared to remain unforgiven;
The wise and the foolish, the guilty and just,
Have quietly mingled their bones in the dust.

"So the multitude goes--like the flower or the weed
That withers away to let others succeed;
So the multitude comes--even those we behold,
To repeat every tale that has often been told:

"For we are the same our fathers have been;
We see the same sights our fathers have seen;
We drink the same stream, we view the same sun,
And run the same course our fathers have run.

"The thoughts we are thinking, our fathers would think;
From the death we are shrinking, our fathers would shrink;
To the life we are clinging, they also would cling—
But it speeds from us all like a bird on the wing.

"They loved--but the story we cannot unfold;
They scorned--but the heart of the haughty is cold;
They grieved--but no wail from their slumber will come;
They joyed--but the tongue of their gladness is dumb.

"They died--aye, they died--and we things that are now,
That walk on the turf that lies o'er their brow,
And make in their dwellings a transient abode,
Meet the things that they met on their pilgrimage road.

"Yea! hope and despondency, pleasure and pain,
Are mingled together in sunshine and rain;
And the smile and the tear, the song and the dirge,
Still follow each other, like surge upon surge.

"'Tis the wink of an eye,--'tis the draught of a breath;--
From the blossom of health to the paleness of death,
From the gilded saloon to the bier and the shroud:--
Oh! why should the spirit of mortal be proud?"

FIVE-LEGGED CALF

President Lincoln had great doubt as to his right to emancipate the slaves under the War power. In discussing the question, he used to like the case to that of the boy who, when asked how many legs his calf would have if he called its tail a leg, replied, "five," to which the prompt response was made that calling the tail a leg would not make it a leg.

A STAGE-COACH STORY

The following is told by Thomas H. Nelson, of Terre Haute, Indiana, who was appointed minister to Chili by Lincoln:

Judge Abram Hammond, afterwards Governor of Indiana, and myself arranged to go from Terre Haute to Indianapolis in a stage-coach.

As we stepped in we discovered that the entire back seat was occupied by a long, lank individual, whose head seemd to protrude from one end of the coach and his feet from the other. He was the sole occupant, and was sleeping soundly. Hammond slapped him familiarly on the shoulder, and asked him if he had chartered the coach that day.

"Certainly not," and he at once took the front seat, politely giving us the place of honor and comfort. An odd-looking fellow he was, with a twenty-five cent hat, without vest or cravat. Regarding him as a good subject for merriment, we perpetrated several jokes.

He took them all with utmost innocence and good nature, and joined in the laugh, although at his own expense.

After an astounding display of wordy pyrotechnics, the dazed and bewildered stranger asked, "What will be the upshot of this comet business?"

Late in the evening we reached Indianapolis, and hurried to Browning's hotel, losing sight of the stranger altogether.

We retired to our room to brush our clothes. In a few minutes I descended to the portico, and there descried our long, gloomy fellow traveler in the center of an admiring group of lawyers, among whom were Judges McLean and Huntington, Albert S. White, and Richard W. Thompson, who seemed to be amused and interested in a story he was telling. I inquired of Browning, the landlord, who he was. "Abraham Lincoln, of Illinois, a member of Congress," was his response.

I was thunderstruck at the announcement. I hastened upstairs and told Hammond the startling news, and together we emerged from the hotel by a back door, and went down an alley to another house, thus avoiding further contact with our distinguished fellow traveler.

Years afterward, when the President-elect was on his way to Washington, I was in the same hotel looking over the distinguished party, when a long arm reached to my shoulder, and a shrill voice exclaimed, "Hello, Nelson! do you think, after all, the whole world is going to follow the darned thing off?" The words were my own in answer to his question in the stage-coach. The speaker was Abraham Lincoln.

ONLY LEVEL-HEADED MEN WANTED

Lincoln wanted men of level heads for important commands. Not infrequently he gave his generals advice.

He appreciated Hooker's bravery, dash and activity, but was fearful of the results of what he denominated "swashing around."

This was one of his telegrams to Hooker:

"And now, beware of rashness; beware of rashness, but, with energy and sleepless vigilance, go forward and give us victories."

HER ONLY IMPERFECTION

At one time a certain Major Hill charged Lincoln with making defamatory remarks regarding Mrs. Hill.

Hill was insulting in his language to Lincoln who never lost his temper.

When he saw his chance to edge a word in, Lincoln denied emphatically using the language or anything like that attributed to him.

He entertained, he insisted, a high regard for Mrs. Hill, and the only thing he knew to her discredit was the fact that she was Major Hill's wife.

HAD TO WAIT FOR HIM

President Lincoln, having arranged to go to New York, was late for his train, much to the disgust of those who were to accompany him, and all were compelled to wait several hours until the next train steamed out of the station. President Lincoln was much amused at the dissatisfaction displayed, and then ventured the remark that the situation reminded him of "a little story." Said he:

"Out in Illinois, a convict who had murdered his cellmate was sentenced to be hanged. On the day set for the execution, crowds lined the roads leading to the spot where the scaffold had been erected, and there was much jostling and excitement. The condemned man took matters coolly, and as one batch of perspiring, anxious men rushed past the cart in which he was riding, he called out, 'Don't be in a hurry, boys. You've got plenty of time. There won't be any fun until I get there.'

"That's the condition of things now," concluded the President; "there won't be any fun at New York until I get there."

TURNED TEARS TO SMILES

One night Schuyler Colfax left all other business to go to the White House to ask the President to respite the son of a constituent, who was sentenced to be shot, at Davenport, for desertion. Mr. Lincoln heard the story with his usual patience, though he was wearied out with incessant calls, and anxious for rest, and then replied:

"Some of our generals complain that I impair discipline and subordination in the army by my pardons and respites, but it makes me rested, after a hard day's work, if I can find some good excuse for saving a man's life, and I go to bed happy as I think how joyous the signing of my name will make him and his family and his friends."

And with a happy smile beaming over that care-furrowed face, he signed that name that saved that life.

WOMEN PLEAD FOR PARDONS

One day during the War an attractively and handsomely dressed woman called on President Lincoln to procure the release from prison of a relation in whom she professed the deepest interest.

She was a good talker, and her winning ways seemed to make a deep impression on the President. After listening to her story, he wrote a few words on a card: "This woman, dear Stanton, is a little smarter than she looks to be," enclosed it in an envelope and directed her to take it to the Secretary of War.

On the same day another woman called, more humble in appearance, more plainly clad. It was the old story.

Father and son both in the army, the former in prison. Could not the latter be discharged from the army and sent home to help his mother?

A few strokes of the pen, a gentle nod of the head, and the little woman, her eyes filling with tears and expressing a grateful acknowledgment her tongue, could not utter, passed out.

A lady so thankful for the release of her husband was in the act of kneeling in thankfulness. "Get up," he said, "don't kneel to me, but thank God and go."

An old lady for the same reason came forward with tears in her eyes to express her gratitude. "Good-bye, Mr. Lincoln," said she; "I shall probably never see you again till we meet in heaven." She had the President's hand in hers, and he was deeply moved. He instantly took her right hand in both of his, and, following her to the door, said, "I am afraid with all my troubles I shall never get to the resting-place you speak of; but if I do, I am sure I shall find you. That you wish me to get there is, I believe, the best wish you could make for me. Good-bye."

Then the President remarked to a friend, "It is more than many can often say, that in doing right one has made two people happy in one day. Speed, die when I may, I want it said of me by those who know me best, that I have always plucked a thistle and planted a flower when I thought a flower would grow."

LINCOLN WISHED TO SEE RICHMOND

The President remarked to Admiral David D. Porter, while on board the flagship Malvern, on the James River, in front of Richmond, the day the city surrendered:

"Thank God that I have lived to see this!

"It seems to me that I have been dreaming a horrid dream for four years, and now the nightmare is gone.

"I wish to see Richmond."

SPOKEN LIKE A CHRISTIAN

Frederick Douglass told, in these words, of his first interview with President Lincoln:

"I approached him with trepidation as to how this great man might receive me; but one word and look from him banished all my fears and set me perfectly at ease. I have often said since that meeting that it was much easier to see and converse with a great man than it was with a small man.

"On that occasion he said:

"'Douglass, you need not tell me who you are. Mr. Seward has told me all about you.'

"I then saw that there was no reason to tell him my personal story, however interesting it might be to myself or others, so I told him at once the object of my visit. It was to get some expression from him upon three points:

"1. Equal pay to colored soldiers.

"2. Their promotion when they had earned it on the battle-field.

"3. Should they be taken prisoners and enslaved or hanged, as Jefferson Davis had threatened, an equal number of Confederate prisoners should be executed within our lines.

"A declaration to that effect I thought would prevent the execution of the rebel threat. To all but the last, President Lincoln assented. He argued, however, that neither equal pay nor promotion could be granted at once. He said that in view of existing prejudices it was a great step forward to employ colored troops at all; that it was necessary to avoid everything that would offend this prejudice and increase opposition to the measure.

"He detailed the steps by which white soldiers were reconciled to the employment of colored troops; how these were first employed as laborers; how it was thought they should not be armed or uniformed like white soldiers; how they should only be made to wear a peculiar uniform; how they should be employed to hold forts and arsenals in sickly locations, and not enter the field like other soldiers.

"With all these restrictions and limitations he easily made me see that much would be gained when the colored man loomed before the country as a full-fledged United States soldier to fight, flourish or fall in defense of the united republic. The great soul of Lincoln halted only when he came to the point of retaliation.

"The thought of hanging men in cold blood, even though the rebels should murder a few of the colored prisoners, was a horror from which he shrank.

"'Oh, Douglass! I cannot do that. If I could get hold of the actual murderers of colored prisoners I would retaliate; but to hang those who have no hand in such murders, I cannot.'

"The contemplation of such an act brought to his countenance such an expression of sadness and pity that it made it hard for me to press my point, though I told him it would tend to save rather than destroy life. He, however, insisted that this work of blood, once begun, would be hard to stop--that such violence would beget violence. He argued more like a disciple of Christ than a commander-in-chief of the army and navy of a warlike nation already involved in a terrible war.

"How sad and strange the fate of this great and good man, the saviour of his country, the embodiment of human charity, whose heart, though strong, was as tender as a heart of childhood; who always tempered justice with mercy; who sought to supplant the sword with counsel of reason, to suppress passion by kindness and moderation; who had a sigh for every human grief and a tear for every human woe, should at last perish by the hand of a desperate assassin, against whom no thought of malice had ever entered his heart!"

"LINCOLN GOES IN WHEN THE QUAKERS ARE OUT"

One of the campaign songs of 1860 which will never be forgotten was Whittier's "The Quakers Are Out:--"

"Give the flags to the winds! Set the hills all aflame! Make way for the man with The Patriarch's name! Away with misgivings--away With all doubt, For Lincoln goes in when the Quakers are out!"

Speaking of this song (with which he was greatly pleased) one day at the White House, the President said: "It reminds me of a little story I heard years ago out in Illinois. A political campaign was on, and the atmosphere was kept at a high temperature. Several fights had already occurred, many men having been seriously hurt, and the prospects were that the result would be close. One of the candidates was a professional politician with a huge wart on his nose, this disfigurement having earned for him the nickname of 'Warty.' His opponent was a young lawyer who wore 'biled' shirts, 'was shaved by a barber, and had his clothes made to fit him.

"Now, 'Warty' was of Quaker stock, and around election time made a great parade of the fact. When there were no campaigns in progress he was anything but Quakerish in his language or actions. The young lawyer didn't know what the inside of a meeting house looked like.

"Well, the night before election-day the two candidates came together at a joint debate, both being on the speakers' platform. The young lawyer had to speak after 'Warty,' and his reputation suffered at the hands of the Quaker, who told the many Friends present what a wicked fellow the young man was--never went to church, swore, drank, smoked and gambled.

"After 'Warty' had finished the other arose and faced the audience. 'I'm not a good man,' said he, 'and what my opponent has said about me is true enough, but I'm always the same. I don't profess religion when I run for office, and then turn around and associate with bad people when the campaign's over. I'm no hypocrite. I don't sing many psalms. Neither does my opponent; and, talking about singing, I'd just like to hear my friend who is running against me sing the song--for the benefit of this audience--I heard him sing the night after he was nominated. I yield the floor to him:

"Of course 'Warty' refused, his Quaker supporters grew suspicious, and when they turned out at the polls the following day they voted for the wicked young lawyer.

"So, it's true that when 'the Quakers are out' the man they support is apt to go in."

HAD CONFIDENCE IN HIM--"BUT--"

"General Blank asks for more men," said Secretary of War Stanton to the President one day, showing the latter a telegram from the

commander named appealing for re-enforcements.

"I guess he's killed off enough men, hasn't he?" queried the President.

"I don't mean Confederates--our own men. What's the use in sending volunteers down to him if they're only used to fill graves?"

"His dispatch seems to imply that, in his opinion, you have not the confidence in him he thinks he deserves," the War Secretary went on to say, as he looked over the telegram again.

"Oh," was the President's reply, "he needn't lose any of his sleep on that account. Just telegraph him to that effect; also, that I don't propose to send him any more men."

HOW HOMINY WAS ORIGINATED

During the progress of a Cabinet meeting the subject of food for the men in the Army happened to come up. From that the conversation changed to the study of the Latin language.

"I studied Latin once," said Mr. Lincoln, in a casual way.

"Were you interested in it?" asked Mr. Seward, the Secretary of State.

"Well, yes. I saw some very curious things," was the President's rejoinder.

"What?" asked Secretary Seward.

"Well, there's the word hominy, for instance. We have just ordered a lot of that stuff for the troops. I see how the word originated. I notice it came from the Latin word homo--a man.

"When we decline homo, it is:

"'Homo--a man.

"'Hominis--of man.

"'Homini--for man.'

"So you see, hominy, being 'for man,' comes from the Latin. I guess those soldiers who don't know Latin will get along with it all right--though I won't rest real easy until I hear from the Commissary Department on it."

HIS IDEA'S OLD, AFTER ALL

One day, while listening to one of the wise men who had called at the White House to unload a large cargo of advice, the President interjected a remark to the effect that he had a great reverence for learning.

"This is not," President Lincoln explained, "because I am not an educated man. I feel the need of reading. It is a loss to a man not to have grown up among books."

"Men of force," the visitor answered, "can get on pretty well without books. They do their own thinking instead of adopting what other men think."

"Yes," said Mr. Lincoln, "but books serve to show a man that those original thoughts of his aren't very new, after all."

This was a point the caller was not willing to debate, and so he cut his call short.

"ABE WANTED NO "SNEAKIN' 'ROUND"

It was in 1830, when "Abe" was just twenty-one years of age, that the Lincoln family moved from Gentryville, Indiana, to near Decatur, Illinois, their household goods being packed in a wagon drawn by four oxen driven by "Abe."

The winter previous the latter had "worked" in a country store in Gentryville and before undertaking the journey he invested all the money he had--some thirty dollars--in notions, such as needles, pins, thread, buttons and other domestic necessities. These he sold to families along the route and made a profit of about one hundred per cent.

This mercantile adventure of his youth "reminded" the President of a very clever story while the members of the Cabinet were one day solemnly debating a rather serious international problem. The President was in the minority, as was frequently the case, and he was "in a hole," as he afterwards expressed it. He didn't want to argue the points raised, preferring to settle the matter in a hurry, and an apt story was his only salvation.

Suddenly the President's fact brightened. "Gentlemen," said he, addressing those seated at the Cabinet table, "the situation just now reminds me of a fix I got into some thirty years or so ago when I was peddling 'notions' on the way from Indiana to Illinois. I didn't have a large stock, but I charged large prices, and I made money. Perhaps you don't see what I am driving at?"

Secretary of State Seward was wearing a most gloomy expression of countenance; Secretary of War Stanton was savage and inclined to be morose; Secretary of the Treasury Chase was indifferent and cynical, while the others of the Presidential advisers resigned themselves to the hearing of the inevitable "story."

"I don't propose to argue this matter," the President went on to say, "because arguments have no effect upon men whose opinions are fixed and whose minds are made up. But this little story of mine will make some things which now are in the dark show up more clearly."

There was another pause, and the Cabinet officers, maintaining their previous silence, began wondering if the President himself really knew what he was "driving at."

"Just before we left Indiana and crossed into Illinois," continued Mr. Lincoln solemnly, speaking in a grave tone of voice, "we came across a small farmhouse full of nothing but children. These ranged in years from seventeen years to seventeen months, and all were in tears. The mother of the family was red-headed and red-faced, and the whip she held in her right hand led to the inference that she had been chastising her brood. The father of the family, a meek-looking, mild-mannered, tow-headed chap, was standing in the front door-way, awaiting--to all appearances--his turn to feel the thong.

"I thought there wasn't much use in asking the head of that house if she wanted any 'notions.' She was too busy. It was evident an insurrection had been in progress, but it was pretty well quelled when I got there. The mother had about suppressed it with an iron hand, but she was not running any risks. She kept a keen and wary eye upon all the children, not forgetting an occasional glance at the 'old man' in the doorway.

"She saw me as I came up, and from her look I thought she was of the opinion that I intended to interfere. Advancing to the doorway, and roughly pushing her husband aside, she demanded my business.

"'Nothing, madame,' I answered as gently as possible; 'I merely dropped in as I came along to see how things were going.'

"'Well, you needn't wait,' was the reply in an irritated way; 'there's trouble here, an' lots of it, too, but I kin manage my own affairs without the help of outsiders. This is jest a family row, but I'll teach these brats their places ef I hev to lick the hide off ev'ry one of them. I don't do much talkin', but I run this house, an' I don't want no one sneakin' round tryin' to find out how I do it, either.'

"That's the case here with us," the President said in conclusion. "We must let the other nations know that we propose to settle our family row in our own way, and 'teach these brats their places' (the seceding States) if we have to 'lick the hide off' of each and every one of them. And, like the old woman, we don't want any 'sneakin' 'round' by other countries who would like to find out how we are to do it, either.

"Now, Seward, you write some diplomatic notes to that effect."

And the Cabinet session closed.

DIDN'T EVEN NEED STILTS

As the President considered it his duty to keep in touch with all the improvements in the armament of the vessels belonging to the United States Navy, he was necessarily interested in the various types of these floating fortresses. Not only was it required of the Navy Department to furnish seagoing warships, deep-draught vessels for the great rivers and the lakes, but this Department also found use for little gunboats which could creep along in the shallowest of water and attack the Confederates in by-places and swamps.

The consequence of the interest taken by Mr. Lincoln in the Navy was that he was besieged, day and night, by steamboat contractors, each one eager to sell his product to the Washington Government. All sorts of experiments were tried, some being dire failures, while others were more than fairly successful. More than once had these tiny war vessels proved themselves of great service, and the United States Government had a large number of them built.

There was one particular contractor who bothered the President more than all the others put together. He was constantly impressing upon Mr. Lincoln the great superiority of his boats, because they would run in such shallow water.

"Oh, yes," replied the President, "I've no doubt they'll run anywhere where the ground is a little moist!"

"HOW DO YOU GET OUT OF THIS PLACE?"

"It seems to me," remarked the President one day while reading, over some of the appealing telegrams sent to the War Department by General McClellan, "that McClellan has been wandering around and has sort of got lost. He's been hollering for help ever since he went South--wants somebody to come to his deliverance and get him out of the place he's got into.

"He reminds me of the story of a man out in Illinois who, in company with a number of friends, visited the State penitentiary. They wandered all through the institution and saw everything, but just about the time to depart this particular man became separated from his friends and couldn't find his way out.

"He roamed up and down one corridor after another, becoming more desperate all the time, when, at last, he came across a convict who was looking out from between the bars of his cell-door. Here was salvation at last. Hurrying up to the prisoner he hastily asked

"'Say! How do you get out of this place?"

"TAD" INTRODUCES "OUR FRIENDS"

President Lincoln often avoided interviews with delegations representing various States, especially when he knew the objects of their errands, and was aware he could not grant their requests. This was the case with several commissioners from Kentucky, who were put off from day to day.

They were about to give up in despair, and were leaving the White House lobby, their speech being interspersed with vehement and uncomplimentary terms concerning "Old Abe," when "Tad" happened along. He caught at these words, and asked one of them if they wanted to see "Old Abe," laughing at the same time.

"Yes," he replied.

"Wait a minute," said "Tad," and rushed into his father's office. Said he, "Papa, may I introduce some friends to you?"

His father, always indulgent and ready to make him happy, kindly said, "Yes, my son, I will see your friends."

"Tad" went to the Kentuckians again, and asked a very dignified looking gentleman of the party his name. He was told his name. He then said, "Come, gentlemen," and they followed him.

Leading them up to the President, "Tad," with much dignity, said, "Papa, let me introduce to you Judge --, of Kentucky;" and quickly added, "Now Judge, you introduce the other gentlemen."

The introductions were gone through with, and they turned out to be the gentlemen Mr. Lincoln had been avoiding for a week. Mr. Lincoln reached for the boy, took him in his lap, kissed him, and told him it was all right, and that he had introduced his friend like a little gentleman as he was. Tad was eleven years old at this time.

The President was pleased with Tad's diplomacy, and often laughed at the incident as he told others of it. One day while caressing the boy, he asked him why he called those gentlemen "his friends." "Well," said Tad, "I had seen them so often, and they looked so good and sorry, and said they were from Kentucky, that I thought they must be our friends." "That is right, my son," said Mr. Lincoln; "I would have the whole human race your friends and mine, if it were possible."

MIXED UP WORSE THAN BEFORE

The President told a story which most beautifully illustrated the muddled situation of affairs at the time McClellan's fate was hanging in the balance. McClellan's s work was not satisfactory, but the

President hesitated to remove him; the general was so slow that the Confederates marched all around him; and, to add to the dilemma, the President could not find a suitable man to take McClellan's place.

The latter was a political, as well as a military, factor; his friends threatened that, if he was removed, many war Democrats would cast their influence with the South, etc. It was, altogether, a sad mix-up, and the President, for a time, was at his wits' end. He was assailed on all sides with advice, but none of it was worth acting upon.

"This situation reminds me," said the President at a Cabinet meeting one day not long before the appointment of General Halleck as McClellan's successor in command of the Union forces, "of a Union man in Kentucky whose two sons enlisted in the Federal Army. His wife was of Confederate sympathies. His nearest neighbor was a Confederate in feeling, and his two sons were fighting under Lee. This neighbor's wife was a Union woman and it nearly broke her heart to know that her sons were arrayed against the Union.

"Finally, the two men, after each had talked the matter over with his wife, agreed to obtain divorces; this they, did, and the Union man and Union woman were wedded, as were the Confederate man and the Confederate woman--the men swapped wives, in short. But this didn't seem to help matters any, for the sons of the Union woman were still fighting for the South, and the sons of the Confederate woman continued in the Federal Army; the Union husband couldn't get along with his Union wife, and the Confederate husband and his Confederate wife couldn't agree upon anything, being forever fussing and quarreling.

"It's the same thing with the Army. It doesn't seem worth while to secure divorces and then marry the Army and McClellan to others, for they won't get along any better than they do now, and there'll only be a new set of heartaches started. I think we'd better wait; perhaps a real fighting general will come along some of these days, and then we'll all be happy. If you go to mixing in a mixup, you only make the muddle worse."

"LONG ABE'S" FEET "PROTRUDED OVER"

George M. Pullman, the great sleeping-car builder, once told a joke in which Lincoln was the prominent figure. In fact, there wouldn't have been any joke had it not been for "Long Abe." At the time of the occurrence, which was the foundation for the joke--and Pullman admitted that the latter was on him--Pullman was the conductor of his only sleeping-car. The latter was an experiment, and Pullman was doing everything possible to get the railroads to take hold of it.

"One night," said Pullman in telling the story, "as we were about going out of Chicago--this was long before Lincoln was what you might call a renowned man--a long, lean, ugly man, with a wart on his cheek, came into the depot. He paid me fifty cents, and half a berth was assigned him. Then he took off his coat and vest and hung them up, and they fitted the peg about as well as they fitted him. Then he kicked off his boots, which were of surprising length, turned into the berth, and, undoubtedly having an easy conscience, was sleeping like a healthy baby before the car left the depot.

"Pretty soon along came another passenger and paid his fifty cents. In two minutes he was back at me, angry as a wet hen.

"'There's a man in that berth of mine,' said he, hotly, 'and he's about ten feet high. How am I going to sleep there, I'd like to know? Go and look at him.'

"In I went--mad, too. The tall, lank man's knees were under his chin, his arms were stretched across the bed and his feet were stored comfortably--for him. I shook him until he awoke, and then told him if he wanted the whole berth he would have to pay $1.

"'My dear sir,' said the tall man, 'a contract is a contract. I have paid you fifty cents for half this berth, and, as you see, I'm occupying it. There's the other half,' pointing to a strip about six inches wide. 'Sell that and don't disturb me again.'

"And so saying, the man with a wart on his face went to sleep again. He was Abraham Lincoln, and he never grew any shorter afterward. We became great friends, and often laughed over the incident."

COULD LICK ANY MAN IN THE CROWD

When the enemies of General Grant were bothering the President with emphatic and repeated demands that the "Silent Man" be removed from command, Mr. Lincoln remained firm. He would not consent to lose the services of so valuable a soldier. "Grant fights," said he in response to the charges made that Grant was a butcher, a drunkard, an incompetent and a general who did not know his business.

"That reminds me of a story," President Lincoln said one day to a delegation of the "Grant-is-no-good" style.

"Out in my State of Illinois there was a man nominated for sheriff of the county. He was a good man for the office, brave, determined and honest, but not much of an orator. In fact, he couldn't talk at all; he couldn't make a speech to save his life.

"His friends knew he was a man who would preserve the peace of the county and perform the duties devolving upon him all right, but the people of the county didn't know it. They wanted him to come out boldly on the platform at political meetings and state his convictions and principles; they had been used to speeches from candidates, and were somewhat suspicious of a man who was afraid to open his mouth.

"At last the candidate consented to make a speech, and his friends were delighted. The candidate was on hand, and, when he was called upon, advanced to the front and faced the crowd. There was a glitter in his eye that wasn't pleasing, and the way he walked out to the front of the stand showed that he knew just what he wanted to say.

"'Feller Citizens,' was his beginning, the words spoken quietly, 'I'm not a speakin' man; I ain't no orator, an' I never stood up before a lot of people in my life before; I'm not goin' to make no speech, 'xcept to say that I can lick any man in the crowd!'"

"LEFT IT THE WOMEN TO HOWL ABOUT ME"

Donn Piatt, one of the brightest newspaper writers in the country, told a good story on the President in regard to the refusal of the latter to sanction the death penalty in cases of desertion from the Union Army.

"There was far more policy in this course," said Piatt, "than kind feeling. To assert the contrary is to detract from Lincoln's force of character, as well as intellect. Our War President was not lost in his high admiration of brigadiers and major-generals, and had a positive dislike for their methods and the despotism upon which an army is based. He knew that he was dependent upon volunteers for soldiers, and to force upon such men as those the stern discipline of the Regular Army was to render the service unpopular. And it pleased him to be the source of mercy, as well as the fountain of honor, in this direction.

"I was sitting with General Dan Tyler, of Connecticut, in the antechamber of the War Department, shortly after the adjournment of the Buell Court of Inquiry, of which we had been members, when President Lincoln came in from the room of Secretary Stanton. Seeing us, he said: 'Well, gentlemen, have you any matter worth reporting?'

"'I think so, Mr. President,' replied General Tyler. 'We had it proven that Bragg, with less than ten thousand men, drove your eighty-three thousand men under Buell back from before Chattanooga, down to the Ohio at Louisville, marched around us twice, then doubled us up at Perryville, and finally got out of the State of Kentucky with all his plunder.'

"'Now, Tyler,' returned the President, 'what is the meaning of all this; what is the lesson? Don't our men march as well, and fight as well, as these rebels? If not, there is a fault somewhere. We are all of the same family--same sort.'

"'Yes, there is a lesson,' replied General Tyler; 'we are of the same sort, but subject to different handling. Bragg's little force was superior to our larger number because he had it under control. If a man left his ranks, he was punished; if he deserted, he was shot. We had nothing of that sort. If we attempt to shoot a deserter you pardon him, and our army is without discipline.'

"The President looked perplexed. 'Why do you interfere?' continued General Tyler. 'Congress has taken from you all responsibility.'

"'Yes,' answered the President impatiently, 'Congress has taken the responsibility and left the women to howl all about me,' and so he strode away."

HE'D RUIN ALL THE OTHER CONVICTS

One of the droll stories brought into play by the President as an ally in support of his contention, proved most effective. Politics was rife among the generals of the Union Army, and there was more "wire-pulling" to prevent the advancement of fellow commanders than the laying of plans to defeat the Confederates in battle.

However, when it so happened that the name of a particularly unpopular general was sent to the Senate for confirmation, the protest against his promotion was almost unanimous. The nomination didn't seem to please anyone. Generals who were enemies before conferred together for the purpose of bringing every possible influence to bear upon the Senate and securing the rejection of the hated leader's name. The President was surprised. He had never known such unanimity before.

"You remind me," said the President to a delegation of officers which called upon him one day to present a fresh protest to him regarding the nomination, "of a visit a certain Governor paid to the Penitentiary of his State. It had been announced that the Governor would hear the story of every inmate of the institution, and was prepared to rectify, either by commutation or pardon, any wrongs that had been done to any prisoner.

"One by one the convicts appeared before His Excellency, and each one maintained that he was an innocent man, who had been sent to prison because the police didn't like him, or his friends and relatives wanted his property, or he was too popular, etc., etc. The last prisoner to appear was an individual who was not all prepossessing. His face was against him; his eyes were shifty; he didn't have the appearance of an honest man, and he didn't act like one.

"'Well,' asked the Governor, impatiently, 'I suppose you're innocent like the rest of these fellows?'

"'No, Governor,' was the unexpected answer; 'I was guilty of the crime they charged against me, and I got just what I deserved.'

"When he had recovered from his astonishment, the Governor, looking the fellow squarely in the face, remarked with emphasis: 'I'll have to pardon you, because I don't want to leave so bad a man as you are in the company of such innocent sufferers as I have discovered your fellow-convicts to be. You might corrupt them and teach them wicked tricks. As soon as I get back to the capital, I'll have the papers made out.'

"You gentlemen," continued the President, "ought to be glad that so bad a man, as you represent this officer to be, is to get his promotion, for then you won't be forced to associate with him and suffer the contamination of his presence and influence. I will do all I can to have the Senate confirm him."

And he was confirmed.

"DID YE ASK MORRISSEY YET?"

John Morrissey, the noted prize fighter, was the "Boss" of Tammany Hall during the Civil War period. It pleased his fancy to go to Congress, and his obedient constituents sent him there. Morrissey was such an absolute despot that the New York City democracy could not make a move without his consent, and many of the Tammanyites were so afraid of him that they would not even enter into business ventures without consulting the autocrat.

President Lincoln had been seriously annoyed by some of his generals, who were afraid to make the slightest move before asking advice from Washington. One commander, in particular, was so cautious that he telegraphed the War Department upon the slightest pretext, the result being that his troops were lying in camp doing nothing, when they should have been in the field.

"This general reminds me," the President said one day while talking to Secretary Stanton, at the War Department, "of a story I once heard about a Tammany man. He happened to meet a friend, also a member of Tammany, on the street, and in the course of the talk the friend, who was beaming with smiles and good nature, told the other Tammanyite that he was going to be married.

"This first Tammany man looked more serious than men usually do upon hearing of the impending happiness of a friend. In fact, his face seemed to take on a look of anxiety and worry.

"'Ain't you glad to know that I'm to get married?' demanded the second Tammanyite, somewhat in a huff.

"'Of course I am,' was the reply; 'but,' putting his mouth close to the ear of the other, 'have ye asked Morrissey yet?'

"Now, this general of whom we are speaking, wouldn't dare order out the guard without asking Morrissey," concluded the President.

GOT THE LAUGH ON DOUGLAS.

At one time, when Lincoln and Douglas were "stumping" Illinois, they met at a certain town, and it was agreed that they would have a joint debate. Douglas was the first speaker, and in the course of his talk remarked that in early life, his father, who, he said, was an excellent cooper by trade, apprenticed him out to learn the cabinet business.

This was too good for Lincoln to let pass, so when his turn came to reply, he said:

"I had understood before that Mr. Douglas had been bound out to learn the cabinet-making business, which is all well enough, but I was not aware until now that his father was a cooper. I have no doubt, however, that he was one, and I am certain, also, that he was a very good one, for (here Lincoln gently bowed toward Douglas) he has made one of the best whiskey casks I have ever seen."

As Douglas was a short heavy-set man, and occasionally imbibed, the pith of the joke was at once apparent, and most heartily enjoyed by all.

On another occasion, Douglas made a point against Lincoln by telling the crowd that when he first knew Lincoln he was a "grocery-keeper," and sold whiskey, cigars, etc.

"Mr. L.," he said, "was a very good bar-tender!" This brought the laugh on Lincoln, whose reply, however, soon came, and then the laugh was on the other side.

"What Mr. Douglas has said, gentlemen," replied Lincoln, "is true enough; I did keep a grocery and I did sell cotton, candles and cigars, and sometimes whiskey; but I remember in those days that Mr. Douglas was one of my best customers."

"I can also say this; that I have since left my side of the counter, while Mr. Douglas still sticks to his!"

This brought such a storm of cheers and laughter that Douglas was unable to reply.

EVEN REBELS OUGHT TO BE SAVED

The Rev. Mr. Shrigley, of Philadelphia, a Universalist, had been nominated for hospital chaplain, and a protesting delegation went to Washington to see President Lincoln on the subject.

"We have called, Mr. President, to confer with you in regard to the appointment of Mr. Shrigley, of Philadelphia, as hospital chaplain."

The President responded: "Oh, yes, gentlemen. I have sent his name to the Senate, and he will no doubt be confirmed at an early date." One of the young men replied: "We have not come to ask for the appointment, but to solicit you to withdraw the nomination."

"Ah!" said Lincoln, "that alters the case; but on what grounds do you wish the nomination withdrawn?"

The answer was: "Mr. Shrigley is not sound in his theological opinions."

The President inquired: "On what question is the gentleman unsound?"

Response: "He does not believe in endless punishment; not only so, sir, but he believes that even the rebels themselves will be finally saved."

"Is that so?" inquired the President.

The members of the committee responded, "Yes, yes.'

"Well, gentlemen, if that be so, and there is any way under Heaven whereby the rebels can be saved, then, for God's sake and their sakes, let the man be appointed."

The Rev. Mr. Shrigley was appointed, and served until the close of the war.

TRIED TO DO WHAT SEEMED BEST.

John M. Palmer, Major-General in the Volunteer Army, Governor of the State of Illinois, and United States Senator from the Sucker State, became acquainted with Lincoln in 1839, and the last time he saw the President was at the White House in February, 1865. Senator Palmer told the story of his interview as follows:

"I had come to Washington at the request of the Governor, to complain that Illinois had been credited with 18,000 too few troops. I saw Mr. Lincoln one afternoon, and he asked me to come again in the morning.

"Next morning I sat in the ante-room while several officers were relieved. At length I was told to enter the President's room. Mr. Lincoln was in the hands of the barber.

"'Come in, Palmer,' he called out, 'come in. You're home folks. I can shave before you. I couldn't before those others, and I have to do it some time.'

"We chatted about various matters, and at length I said:

"'Well, Mr. Lincoln, if anybody had told me that in a great crisis like this the people were going out to a little one-horse town and pick out a one-horse lawyer for President I wouldn't have believed it.'

"Mr. Lincoln whirled about in his chair, his face white with lather, a towel under his chin. At first I thought he was angry. Sweeping the barber away he leaned forward, and, placing one hand on my knee, said:

"'Neither would I. But it was time when a man with a policy would have been fatal to the country. I have never had a policy. I have simply tried to do what seemed best each day, as each day came.'"

NASHVILLE WAS NOT SURRENDERED

"I was told a mighty good story," said the President one day at a Cabinet meeting, "by Colonel Granville Moody, 'the fighting Methodist parson,' as they used to call him in Tennessee. I happened to meet Moody in Philadelphia, where he was attending a conference.

"The story was about 'Andy' Johnson and General Buell. Colonel Moody happened to be in Nashville the day it was reported that Buell had decided to evacuate the city. The rebels, strongly re-inforced, were said to be within two days' march of the capital. Of course, the city was greatly excited. Moody said he went in search of Johnson at the edge of the evening and found him at his office closeted with two gentlemen, who were walking the floor with him, one on each side. As he entered they retired, leaving him alone with Johnson, who came up to him, manifesting intense feeling, and said:

"'Moody, we are sold out. Buell is a traitor. He is going to evacuate the city, and in forty-eight hours we will all be in the hands of the rebels!'

"Then he commenced pacing the floor again, twisting his hands and chafing like a caged tiger, utterly insensible to his friend's entreaties to become calm. Suddenly he turned and said:

"'Moody, can you pray?'

"'That is my business, sir, as a minister of the gospel,' returned the colonel.

"'Well, Moody, I wish you would pray,' said Johnson, and instantly both went down upon their knees at opposite sides of the room.

"As the prayer waxed fervent, Johnson began to respond in true Methodist style. Presently he crawled over on his hands and knees to Moody's side and put his arms over him, manifesting the deepest emotion.

"Closing the prayer with a hearty 'amen' from each, they arose.

"Johnson took a long breath, and said, with emphasis:

"'Moody, I feel better.'

"Shortly afterward he asked:

"'Will you stand by me?'

"'Certainly I will,' was the answer.

"'Well, Moody, I can depend upon you; you are one in a hundred thousand.'

"He then commenced pacing the floor again. Suddenly he wheeled, the current of his thought having changed, and said:

"'Oh, Moody, I don't want you to think I have become a religious man because I asked you to pray. I am sorry to say it, I am not, and never pretended to be religious. No one knows this better than you, but, Moody, there is one thing about it, I do believe in Almighty God, and I believe also in the Bible, and I say, d--n me if Nashville shall be surrendered!'

"And Nashville was not surrendered!"

HE COULDN'T WAIT FOR THE COLONEL

General Fisk, attending a reception at the White House, saw waiting in the ante-room a poor old man from Tennessee, and learned that he had been waiting three or four days to get an audience, on which probably depended the life of his son, under sentence of death for some military offense.

General Fisk wrote his case in outline on a card and sent it in, with a a special request that the President would see the man. In a moment the order came; and past impatient senators, governors and generals, the old man went.

He showed his papers to Mr. Lincoln, who said he would look into the case and give him the result next day.

The old man, in an agony of apprehension, looked up into the President's sympathetic face and actually cried out:

"To-morrow may be too late! My son is under sentence of death! It ought to be decided now!"

His streaming tears told how much he was moved.

"Come," said Mr. Lincoln, "wait a bit and I'll tell you a story;" and then he told the old man General Fisk's story about the swearing driver, as follows:

"The general had begun his military life as a colonel, and when he raised his regiment in Missouri he proposed to his men that he should do all the swearing of the regiment. They assented; and for months no instance was known of the violation of the promise.

"The colonel had a teamster named John Todd, who, as roads were not always the best, had some difficulty in commanding his temper and his tongue.

"John happened to be driving a mule team through a series of mudholes a little worse than usual, when, unable to restrain himself any longer, he burst forth into a volley of energetic oaths.

"The colonel took notice of the offense and brought John to account.

"'John,' said he, 'didn't you promise to let me do all the swearing of the regiment?'

"'Yes, I did, colonel,' he replied, 'but the fact was, the swearing had to be done then or not at all, and you weren't there to do it.'"

As he told the story the old man forgot his boy, and both the President and his listener had a hearty laugh together at its conclusion.

Then he wrote a few words which the old man read, and in which he found new occasion for tears; but the tears were tears of joy, for the words saved the life of his son.

LINCOLN PRONOUNCED THIS STORY FUNNY

The President was heard to declare one day that the story given below was one of the funniest he ever heard.

One of General Fremont's batteries of eight Parrott guns, supported by a squadron of horse commanded by Major Richards, was in sharp conflict with a battery of the enemy near at hand. Shells and shot were flying thick and fast, when the commander of the battery, a German, one of Fremont's staff, rode suddenly up to the cavalry, exclaiming, in loud and excited terms, "Pring up de shackasses! Pring up de shackasses! For Cot's sake, hurry up de shackasses, im-me-di-ate-ly!"

The necessity of this order, though not quite apparent, will be more obvious when it is remembered that "shackasses" are mules, carry mountain howitzers, which are fired from the backs of that much-abused but valuable animal; and the immediate occasion for the "shackasses" was that two regiments of rebel infantry were at that moment discovered ascending a hill immediately behind our batteries.

The "shackasses," with the howitzers loaded with grape and canister, were soon on the ground.

The mules squared themselves, as they well knew how, for the shock.

A terrific volley was poured into the advancing column, which immediately broke and retreated.

Two hundred and seventy-eight dead bodies were found in the ravine next day, piled closely together as they fell, the effects of that volley from the backs of the "shackasses."

JOKE WAS ON LINCOLN

Mr. Lincoln enjoyed a joke at his own expense. Said he: "In the days when I used to be in the circuit, I was accosted in the cars by a stranger, who said, 'Excuse me, sir, but I have an article in my possession which belongs to you.' 'How is that?' I asked, considerably astonished.

"The stranger took a jackknife from his pocket. 'This knife,' said he, 'was placed in my hands some years ago, with the injunction that I was to keep it until I had found a man uglier than myself. I have carried it from that time to this. Allow me to say, sir, that I think you are fairly entitled to the property.'"

THE OTHER ONE WAS WORSE

It so happened that an official of the War Department had escaped serious punishment for a rather flagrant offense, by showing where grosser irregularities existed in the management of a certain bureau of the Department. So valuable was the information furnished that the culprit who "gave the snap away" was not even discharged.

"That reminds me," the President said, when the case was laid before him, "of a story about Daniel Webster, when the latter was a boy.

"When quite young, at school, Daniel was one day guilty of a gross violation of the rules. He was detected in the act, and called up by the teacher for punishment.

"This was to be the old-fashioned 'feruling' of the hand. His hands happened to be very dirty.

"Knowing this, on the way to the teacher's desk, he spit upon the palm of his right hand, wiping it off upon the side of his pantaloons.

"'Give me your hand, sir,' said the teacher, very sternly.

"Out went the right hand, partly cleansed. The teacher looked at it a moment, and said:

"'Daniel, if you will find another hand in this school-room as filthy as that, I will let you off this time!'

"Instantly from behind the back came the left hand.

"'Here it is, sir,' was the ready reply.

"'That will do,' said the teacher, 'for this time; you can take your seat, sir.'"

"I'D A BEEN MISSED BY MYSE'F"

The President did not consider that every soldier who ran away in battle, or did not stand firmly to receive a bayonet charge, was a coward. He was of opinion that self-preservation was the first law of Nature, but he didn't want this statute construed too liberally by the troops.

At the same time he took occasion to illustrate a point he wished to make by a story in connection with a darky who was a member of the Ninth Illinois Infantry Regiment. This regiment was one of those engaged at the capture of Fort Donelson. It behaved gallantly, and lost as heavily as any.

"Upon the hurricane-deck of one of our gunboats," said the President in telling the story, "I saw an elderly darky, with a very philosophical and retrospective cast of countenance, squatted upon his bundle, toasting his shins against the chimney, and apparently plunged into a state of profound meditation.

"As the negro rather interested me, I made some inquiries, and found that he had really been with the Ninth Illinois Infantry at Donelson. and began to ask him some questions about the capture of the place.

"'Were you in the fight?'

"'Had a little taste of it, sa.'

"'Stood your ground, did you?'

"'No, sa, I runs.'

"'Run at the first fire, did you?

"'Yes, sa, and would hab run soona, had I knowd it war comin'."

"'Why, that wasn't very creditable to your courage.'

"'Dat isn't my line, sa--cookin's my profeshun.'

"'Well, but have you no regard for your reputation?'

"'Reputation's nuffin to me by de side ob life.'

"'Do you consider your life worth more than other people's?'

"'It's worth more to me, sa.'

"'Then you must value it very highly?'

"'Yes, sa, I does, more dan all dis wuld, more dan a million ob dollars, sa, for what would dat be wuth to a man wid de bref out ob him? Self-preserbation am de fust law wid me.'

"'But why should you act upon a different rule from other men?'

"'Different men set different values on their lives; mine is not in de market.'

"'But if you lost it you would have the satisfaction of knowing that you died for your country.'

"'Dat no satisfaction when feelin's gone.'

"'Then patriotism and honor are nothing to you?'

"'Nufin whatever, sat--I regard them as among the vanities.'

"'If our soldiers were like you, traitors might have broken up the government without resistance.'

"'Yes, sa, dar would hab been no help for it. I wouldn't put my life in de scale 'g'inst any gobernment dat eber existed, for no gobernment could replace de loss to me.'

"'Do you think any of your company would have missed you if you had been killed?'

"'Maybe not, sa--a dead white man ain't much to dese sogers, let alone a dead nigga--but I'd a missed myse'f, and dat was de p'int wid me.'

"I only tell this story," concluded the President, "in order to illustrate the result of the tactics of some of the Union generals who would be sadly 'missed' by themselves, if no one else, if they ever got out of the Army."

IT ALL "DEPENDED" UPON THE EFFECT

President Lincoln and some members of his Cabinet were with a part of the Army some distance south of the National Capital at one time, when Secretary of War Stanton remarked that just before he left Washington he had received a telegram from General Mitchell, in Alabama. General Mitchell asked instructions in regard to a certain emergency that had arisen.

The Secretary said he did not precisely understand the emergency as explained by General Mitchell, but had answered back, "All right; go ahead."

"Now," he said, as he turned to Mr. Lincoln, "Mr. President, if I have made an error in not understanding him correctly, I will have to get you to countermand the order."

"Well," exclaimed President Lincoln, "that is very much like the happening on the occasion of a certain horse sale I remember that took place at the cross-roads down in Kentucky, when I was a boy.

"A particularly fine horse was to be sold, and the people in large numbers had gathered together. They had a small boy to ride the horse up and down while the spectators examined the horse's points.

"At last one man whispered to the boy as he went by: 'Look here, boy, hain't that horse got the splints?'

"The boy replied: 'Mister, I don't know what the splints is, but if it's good for him, he has got it; if it ain't good for him, he ain't got it.'

"Now," said President Lincoln, "if this was good for Mitchell, it was all right; but if it was not, I have got to countermand it."

TOO SWIFT TO STAY IN THE ARMY

There were strange, queer, odd things and happenings in the Army at times, but, as a rule, the President did not allow them to worry him. He had enough to bother about.

A quartermaster having neglected to present his accounts in proper shape, and the matter being deemed of sufficient importance to bring it to the attention of the President, the latter remarked:

"Now this instance reminds me of a little story I heard only a short time ago. A certain general's purse was getting low, and he said it was probable he might be obliged to draw on his banker for some money.

"'How much do you want, father?' asked his son, who had been with him a few days.

"'I think I shall send for a couple of hundred,' replied the general.

"Why, father,' said his son, very quietly, 'I can let you have it.'

"'You can let me have it! Where did you get so much money?

"'I won it playing draw-poker with your staff, sir!' replied the youth.

"The earliest morning train bore the young man toward his home, and I've been wondering if that boy and that quartermaster had happened to meet at the same table."

ADMIRED THE STRONG MAN

Governor Hoyt of Wisconsin tells a story of Mr. Lincoln's great admiration for physical strength. Mr. Lincoln, in 1859, made a speech at the Wisconsin State Agricultural Fair. After the speech, in company with the Governor, he strolled about the grounds, looking at the exhibits. They came to a place where a professional "strong man" was tossing cannon balls in the air and catching them on his arms and juggling with them as though they were light as baseballs. Mr. Lincoln had never before seen such an exhibition, and he was greatly surprised and interested.

When the performance was over, Governor Hoyt, seeing Mr. Lincoln's interest, asked him to go up and be introduced to the athlete. He did so, and, as he stood looking down musingly on the man, who was very short, and evidently wondering that one so much smaller than he could be so much stronger, he suddenly broke out with one of his quaint speeches. "Why," he said, "why, I could lick salt off the top of your hat."

WISHED THE ARMY CHARGED LIKE THAT

A prominent volunteer officer who, early in the War, was on duty in Washington and often carried reports to Secretary Stanton at the War Department, told a characteristic story on President Lincoln. Said he:

"I was with several other young officers, also carrying reports to the War Department, and one morning we were late. In this instance we were in a desperate hurry to deliver the papers, in order to be able to catch the train returning to camp.

"On the winding, dark staircase of the old War Department, which many will remember, it was our misfortune, while taking about three stairs at a time, to run a certain head like a catapult into the body of the President, striking him in the region of the right lower vest pocket.

"The usual surprised and relaxed grunt of a man thus assailed came promptly.

"We quickly sent an apology in the direction of the dimly seen form, feeling that the ungracious shock was expensive, even to the humblest clerk in the department.

"A second glance revealed to us the President as the victim of the collision. Then followed a special tender of 'ten thousand pardons,' and the President's reply:

"'One's enough; I wish the whole army would charge like that.'"

"UNCLE ABRAHAM" HAD EVERYTHING READY

"You can't do anything with them Southern fellows," the old man at the table was saying.

"If they get whipped, they'll retreat to them Southern swamps and bayous along with the fishes and crocodiles. You haven't got the fish-nets made that'll catch 'em."

"Look here, old gentleman," remarked President Lincoln, who was sitting alongside, "we've got just the nets for traitors, in the bayous or anywhere."

"Hey? What nets?"

"Bayou-nets!" and "Uncle Abraham" pointed his joke with his fork, spearing a fishball savagely.

NOT AS SMOOTH AS HE LOOKED

Mr. Lincoln's skill in parrying troublesome questions was wonderful. Once he received a call from Congressman John Ganson, of Buffalo, one of the ablest lawyers in New York, who, although a Democrat, supported all of Mr. Lincoln's war measures. Mr. Ganson wanted explanations. Mr. Ganson was very bald with a perfectly smooth face. He had a most direct and aggressive way of stating his views or of demanding what he thought he was entitled to. He said: "Mr. Lincoln, I have supported all of your measures and think I am entitled to your confidence. We are voting and acting in the dark in Congress, and I demand to know--think I have the right to ask and to know--what is the present situation, and what are the prospects and conditions of the several campaigns and armies."

Mr. Lincoln looked at him critically for a moment and then said: "Ganson, how clean you shave!"

Most men would have been offended, but Ganson was too broad and intelligent a man not to see the point and retire at once, satisfied, from the field.

A SMALL CROP.

Chauncey M. Depew says that Mr. Lincoln told him the following story, which he claimed was one of the best two things he ever originated: He was trying a case in Illinois where he appeared for a prisoner charged with aggravated assault and battery. The complainant had told a horrible story of the attack, which his appearance fully justified, when the District Attorney handed the witness over to Mr. Lincoln, for cross-examination. Mr. Lincoln said he had no testimony, and unless he could break down the complainant's story he saw no way out. He had come to the conclusion that the witness was a bumptious man, who rather prided himself upon his smartness in repartee and, so, after looking at him for some minutes, he said:

"Well, my friend, how much ground did you and my client here fight over?"

The fellow answered: "About six acres."

"Well," said Mr. Lincoln, "don't you think that this is an almighty small crop of fight to gather from such a big piece of ground?"

The jury laughed. The Court and District-Attorney and complainant all joined in, and the case was laughed out of court.

"NEVER REGRET WHAT YOU DON'T WRITE"

A simple remark one of the party might make would remind Mr. Lincoln of an apropos story.

Secretary of the Treasury Chase happened to remark, "Oh, I am so sorry that I did not write a letter to Mr. So-and-so before I left home!"

President Lincoln promptly responded:

"Chase, never regret what you don't write; it is what you do write that you are often called upon to feel sorry for."

A VAIN GENERAL

In an interview between President Lincoln and Petroleum V. Nasby, the name came up of a recently deceased politician of Illinois whose merit was blemished by great vanity. His funeral was very largely attended.

"If General --- had known how big a funeral he would have had," said Mr. Lincoln, "he would have died years ago."

DEATH BED REPENTANCE

A Senator, who was calling upon Mr. Lincoln, mentioned the name of a most virulent and dishonest official; one, who, though very brilliant, was very bad.

"It's a good thing for B---" said Mr. Lincoln. "that there is such a thing as a deathbed repentance."

NO CAUSE FOR PRIDE

A member of Congress from Ohio came into Mr. Lincoln's presence in a state of unutterable intoxication, and sinking into a chair, exclaimed in tones that welled up fuzzy through the gallon or more of whiskey that he contained, "Oh, 'why should (hic) the spirit of mortal be proud?'"

"My dear sir," said the President, regarding him closely, "I see no reason whatever."

HOW "JAKE" GOT AWAY

One of the last, if not the very last story told by President Lincoln, was to one of his Cabinet who came to see him, to ask if it would be proper to permit "Jake" Thompson to slip through Maine in disguise and embark for Portland.

The President, as usual, was disposed to be merciful, and to permit the arch-rebel to pass unmolested, but Secretary Stanton urged that he should be arrested as a traitor.

"By permitting him to escape the penalties of treason," persisted the War Secretary, "you sanction it."

"Well," replied Mr. Lincoln, "let me tell you a story. There was an Irish soldier here last summer, who wanted something to drink stronger than water, and stopped at a drug-shop, where he espied a soda-fountain. 'Mr. Doctor,' said he, 'give me, plase, a glass of soda-wather, an' if yez can put in a few drops of whiskey unbeknown to any one, I'll be obleeged.' Now, continued Mr. Lincoln, "if 'Jake' Thompson is permitted to go through Maine unbeknown to any one, what's the harm? So don't have him arrested."

MARY TODD LINCOLN'S OPINION OF HER HUSBAND

In Lincoln's struggles, both in the law and for political advancement, his wife shared his sacrifices. She was a plucky little woman, and in fact endowed with a more restless ambition than he. She was gifted with a rare insight into the motives that actuate mankind, and there is no doubt that much of Lincoln's success was in a measure attributable to her acuteness and the stimulus of her influence.

His election to Congress within four years after their marriage afforded her extreme gratification. She loved power and prominence, and was inordinately proud of her tall and ungainly husband. She saw in him bright prospects ahead, and his every move was watched by her with the closest interest. If to other persons he seemed homely, to her he was the embodiment of noble manhood, and each succeeding day impressed upon her the wisdom of her choice of Lincoln over Douglas--if in reality she ever seriously accepted the latter's attentions.

"Mr. Lincoln may not be as handsome a figure," she said one day in Lincoln's law office during her husband's absence, when the conversation turned on Douglas, "but the people are perhaps not aware that his heart is as large as his arms are long."

www.ingramcontent.com/pod-product-compliance
Lightning Source LLC
Chambersburg PA
CBHW031244290426
44109CB00012B/431